"THE HIGHER CHRISTIAN LIFE"

SOURCES FOR THE STUDY OF THE HOLINESS, PENTECOSTAL, AND KESWICK MOVEMENTS

A forty-eight-volume facsimile series reprinting extremely rare documents for the study of nineteenth-century religious and social history, the rise of feminism, and the history of the Pentecostal and Charismatic movements

Edited by

Donald W. Dayton
Northern Baptist Theological Seminary

Advisory Editors

D. William Faupel, *Asbury Theological Seminary*
Cecil M. Robeck, Jr., *Fuller Theological Seminary*
Gerald T. Sheppard, *Union Theological Seminary*

A GARLAND SERIES

AUTOBIOGRAPHY OF THE REV. LUTHER LEE

Garland Publishing, Inc.
New York & London
1984

For a complete list of the titles in this series
see the final pages of this volume.

This facsimile has been made from a copy in
the Yale Divinity School Library.

Library of Congress Cataloging in Publication Data

Lee, Luther, 1800–1889.
Autobiography of the Rev. Luther Lee.

(The Higher Christian life")
Reprint. Originally published: New York :
Phillips & Hunt, 1882.
1. Lee, Luther, 1800–1889.   2. Methodist Church—
United States—Clergy—Biography.   I. Title.   II. Series.
BX8495.L45A3   1984   287'.1'0924 [B]   84-18827
ISBN 0-8240-6426-7 (alk. paper)

The volumes in this series are printed on
acid-free, 250-year-life paper.

Printed in the United States of America

AUTOBIOGRAPHY

OF THE

REV. LUTHER LEE, D.D.

"Strike, but hear me."

NEW YORK:

PHILLIPS & HUNT.

CINCINNATI:

WALDEN & STOWE.

1882.

PREFACE.

IN presenting the following pages to the public I believe myself to be offering that which will be both entertaining and useful. The scene does not open under the shadow of a throne surrounded by the curtains of royalty, nor amid the political machinery that always has and always will gather around the center of a republic to fatten upon its spoils and shape its destiny. It opens with the cloudy dawn of an obscure beginning, and unfolds amid the scenes of rural and unsophisticated life before what is called modern improvements, like a wave, swept over the land, and changed the face of society. Rural society seventy years ago was a very different thing from what it is to-day, and in no aspect has it changed more than in the morals and religion of the several denominations of Christians, and in their relations to each other. Many things which were then considered as right are now denounced as the most flagitious crimes, and denominations which then made war upon each other and denounced each other as damnable heretics now co-operate and sing and pray together as loving Christian brethren. Some persons of the present day appear to suppose themselves living in a degenerate age. If such will read the following pages it may tinge their gloomy thoughts with some brighter rays, if it does not lift the cloud entirely from their minds.

The writer's memory, like a telescopic view, sweeps the fields of seventy years, and he can appreciate things as they were and as they are, having witnessed all the changes which have culminated in the present condition of society. The age in which the writer has lived has been the most distinguished for human progress of all the ages since time dawned. Of course no general history of the times will be attempted; the writer will confine himself mainly to his own limited circle; but the incidents of his life which may be narrated will be largely representative and highly suggestive, giving a clear insight into those long-departed years over which the flight of time is fast spreading the deepening vail of oblivion.

There are now living but very few persons who were born with the century, and who were pioneers in the great movements which have distinguished it from all other centuries. The writer must soon pass away, but before his long active brain and hand cease their functions he wishes to make a record of his times which may remain, and act for a time, at least, after his personal work is finished. Some of the most important theological ques-tions which were discussed and settled fifty years ago are being opened again for re-exami.nation. As the writer had a large share in the discussions of those times, a brief state-ment of the questions as then controverted and settled cannot fail to be interesting, and may save some labor to the disputants of the present day. Truth is the same now that it was then, and, in the main, the same arguments which were successful in the defense of truth then will prove successful still if properly applied.

The fact that the Churches and ministers largely took the wrong side in the early discussion of the subject of slavery has passed into history, and this volume is not intended to add to that general history, but only to show the part the writer had in furnishing the facts of that history, having taken a very active part in the antislavery discussion. So large a portion of the writer's life was devoted to the antislavery cause that his biography would be defective and false if this were omitted.

With these brief explanations the narrative is submitted to a generous public.

LUTHER LEE.

FLINT, MICHIGAN, *October*, 1881.

CONTENTS.

———•———

CHAPTER I.

CHAPTER XV.

CHAPTER XVI.

CHAPTER XVII.

CHAPTER XVIII.

CHAPTER XIX.

CHAPTER XX.

CHAPTER XXVIII.

CHAPTER XXIX.

CHAPTER XXX.

CHAPTER XXXI.

CHAPTER XXXII.

CHAPTER XXXIII.

CHAPTER XXXIV.

AUTOBIOGRAPHY

OF

REV. LUTHER LEE.

CHAPTER I.

My Parentage.

I AM unable to trace an ancestral line beyond grandparents. I am of pure English descent. My grandfather Lee was an Englishman, and came to Boston about 1748 or 1750. He married Miss Deborah Bundy. Their union was blessed with two sons, Samuel and Moses. Samuel, the oldest, was my father. He was born in 1754, and, consequently, was twenty-one years old at the commencement of the Revolution, when he enlisted, and served his country until he was discharged after our independence was acknowledged.

My mother's maiden name was Williams. Her father was an Englishman, and came to America as a soldier under General Braddock, and was in the disastrous battle of Braddock's defeat. When discharged from the army he went to Connecticut, and settled in Woodbury, on Lord Woodbury's Patent. Woodbury was afterward called Bethlehem. He married

Miss Thankful Spencer, of the Puritan stock. Their daughter Hannah was my mother. Grandfather Williams died when he was young, and she was brought up in the family of the Rev. Dr. Belamy, the great New England divine of that day.

When my father was discharged from the army, at the close of the Revolution, he found his way to Woodbury, Conn., and married Miss Hannah Williams, who was still living in the family of Dr. Belamy. Nine children were the result of their union, all of whom lived to be men and women. We were a family of seven brothers and two sisters, of which I was the youngest save one. I am the only one left of the nine. The youngest died at the age of fifty, about twenty-eight years ago; and my oldest brother, and the oldest of the family, died about seven years ago, at the advanced age of ninety-one; and I am the last of the family lingering on these shores of mortality, now in my eighty-first year.

CHAPTER II.

My Childhood and Youth.

I WAS born in Schoharie, N. Y., but my parents moved into Delaware County at the dawn of my recollection. Memory made its first clear and indelible record in the township of Courtwright. This was the neighborhood of the distinguished Bangs family, some of whom I remember very distinctly. John Bangs held meetings in my father's house when I was seven or eight years old, and I remember to have been affected by his very loud and earnest exhortation.

I removed with my parents into Ulster County when I was about nine years old. At the age of thirteen I lost my mother, and the family was broken up ; and I found myself alone in the world, and, under God, I have been my own guardian and caretaker ever since.

No one who has not been in like circumstances can know the utter loneliness and desolation which I then felt ; and the years that followed, until I became a man, were the saddest years of all my life. I am not sure that they have not left an impression on my mind which will modify the whole of my subsequent existence.

After serious thought and revolving in my mind the best course to pursue, I set my young face westward, and struck out for a new home to be sought among strangers. This was in Ulster County, and the principal road leading north-west was known as the Old Esopus Turnpike, called Sopus in common parlance. This road led me over Pine Hill, so-called, but more properly Hemlock Mountain, and after crossing the mountain I descended into the valley of the east branch of the Delaware River, and made my first stand in Middletown, Delaware County.

It was in the month of April, and I hired myself out for the summer. In the fall, when my contract was finished, I went to live with a man by the name of Smith, the next neighbor, with whom I had formed a favorable acquaintance during the summer. Mr. Smith owned a custom grist-mill, with a single run of stones, in which all kinds of grain were ground. I soon learned to grind, and became master of the establishment, and had principal charge of it while I remained in Mr. Smith's employ, which was about four years.

I found that same Mr. Smith in Michigan, near Addison, in 1864, forty-nine years after I left his service, having never seen him or heard from him during all these years. At the time I found him he was over eighty years old.

I left Mr. Smith in the fall of 1817, and went to

live with Mr. Daniel H. Burr, only about four miles distant. I had done the grinding for Mr. Burr for a number of years, and hence had become well acquainted with him. Learning that I was a little dissatisfied with my position, Mr. Burr made me an offer to come and live with him until I should be twenty-one, and I took him at his offer and closed the bargain, and we both fulfilled our contract to the word. I cannot say to the letter, for no papers were executed between us. Mr. Burr was a farmer on a small scale, and also a tanner or leather-maker on a small scale ; and I worked at both as circumstances required. As a man Mr. Burr was honest and honorable, and I never had occasion to complain of his personal treatment ; yet he was in belief a Deist. He believed in God and Providence, but he did not believe in Christ nor in the inspiration of the Scriptures.

There were no religious meetings nearer than five miles in one direction and six in another. There were no professors in the neighborhood, and, of course, I was under the pressure of no external religious influence. I, however, embraced religion before I left Mr. Burr, as will be related in the following chapter. There was but little regard for morality in the community, and drinking and even drunkenness were very common. And though for a time I fell into some of the immoral habits of the neighborhood, such as a disregard of the Sabbath, I never committed the folly and crime of drinking, and was never drunk in my life. I now look upon it as strange that I was never induced to drink with drinking associates all around me, and I thank God for his preserving care; for it seems that nothing else could have held me back from the grosser vices which were openly practiced all around me.

CHAPTER III.

My Early Religious Experience.

MY first remembered religious feeling transpired when I was about eight years old. My mother was a Methodist, and listening to her reading the narrative of the Rev. Freeborn Garrettson, I was moved to tears, especially by some of the scenes of persecution through which he passed, and I hid my face so that no one should see that I was weeping. I then had an impression that I should be a preacher. That impression never left me, nor was I ever after without religious feeling, which was often roused almost to the point of open development; yet such were my external surroundings that I was prevented from taking any religious stand until I was nineteen years old. I had then attained more courage, and a more independent state of mind, so that, notwithstanding the outside pressure of skepticism and irreligion with which I was surrounded, my religious feeling took on an outward form, and I went to the nearest preaching place on old Delaware Circuit, and joined the Methodist Episcopal Church, and took upon myself her solemn baptismal vows. That was an epoch in my life, a turning-point, the beginning of a brighter future. To be sure, the future was not bright to my view. As yet I had no plan of life; mist and darkness hung on my path; but a hope was kindled and an energy roused within me never experienced before, and I felt, and could not help feeling, I had something to live for more than I had ever realized before. What it was was yet vague, and how it was to be realized not yet conceived, but I was roused to greater mental activity, and that was something toward reaching an end. My active mind was not slow in giving external forms to thoughts that struggled and burned within, as will be seen; and this mental operation was soon aided by suggestions, as my connection with the Church placed me in new associations, and brought around me an entirely new and different class of friends. I entered upon my Christian life, after joining the Church and taking upon myself the obligations of a baptized Christian, with no other plan than to do my Christian duty and honor the profession I had made. In pursuance of this purpose, though very timid, I soon learned to take part in social and public meetings as opportunities occurred and duty seemed to demand, and I often prayed and spoke in meetings, in common with others; and such were the Christian smiles that beamed on me, such the warm shake of the hand and the encouraging tap on the shoulder that I received from the older members of the Church, that my very great diffidence was rapidly overcome, and my advancement in a religious life appeared to others to be rapid, as I can now judge from the pleasant memory I have of their kind words and demeanor toward me.

It was not long before some of the leading members of the Church saw, or thought they saw, in me a promise of future usefulness, and they managed, in their cautious way, to encourage me, and to draw me out in the public exercise of my gifts, and they were quite successful. I can see it all plainly now, but then, in my inexperience and simplicity, I did not understand it. Things went on in this way, and I attended meetings all I could, until November 25, just six days before I was twenty-one years old. On this day I went to meeting at the usual place of preaching, which was in the private dwelling of the old Dutch class-leader, Jacob Duboys, whose house stood on the bank of the Delaware River, in the town of Andes. The preacher did not make his appearance, and, after waiting a reasonable time, the old leader, who could never give the sound of the th, came to me and said, "Broder Luter, you must talk to the people." I was frightened, and trembled in every limb, yet I did not dare to refuse, and, stepping forward, I made my first attempt to preach. I apprehend it was not much of a sermon, but it was a beginning, and met with such approval, and brought to me such encouragement, that I continued to exercise my gifts, and have done so ever since, now sixty years. There was great want of laborers, and when the people learned that I could talk, I had invitations enough, and it was thought that I made rapid improvement. My first written license was signed by the Rev. Eben Smith, who was presiding elder on the Hudson River District at that time. Delaware Circuit was a part of the district, and embraced the whole of Delaware County, and extended into two or three other counties, and how much more I cannot say; but I remember very distinctly that it was more than three hundred miles around it, which required seventy-five miles travel a week, on an average, and a fraction over ten miles a day. Such a field of labor, spreading over such a wild country as Delaware County was then, left ample room for the exercise of all the gifts found among the wide-spread and scattered people, and I always had enough to do while I remained in that mountainous country, with its lofty hill-tops and deep glens and coves, many of which the circuit preachers were compelled to pass by for want of time.

CHAPTER IV.

My Career as a Local Preacher.

THIS will constitute a short chapter, as there is but little of note to be told of this period of my life, which embraced nearly seven years. I was uneducated and inexperienced, and I commenced my public life under disadvantages which cannot be understood by those who have been schooled from childhood, and have been reared to manhood by Christian parents and received good home-training. None of these advantages had been mine. New York had no common-school law when I was a child, and there were no schools in the backgrounds then, where an all-wise and just Providence gave me my childhood existence. I had an older brother, who had been schooled before my parents moved into the new section where I began to think and act. That brother cut the letters of the alphabet with his penknife upon a pine shingle, and thus I learned my letters, and that was the humble beginning of my education. I soon learned the sound of the letters, and how to combine them so as to spell "ba, be, bi, bo, bu, by." That same brother, at a later period, secured for me the "American Spelling-book," and I learned to read its easy lessons, and during my minority became able to read the Bible and hymn book, to write a little, and to work in figures as far as division, and all this without going to school. This, perhaps, was in advance of the average of my associates, for education was not within reach of the humble, and was not appreciated. When I was nineteen years old I remember to have been heartily laughed at, and even ridiculed, for my honest declaration that I meant yet, at some future period, to understand grammar. I nevertheless reached that goal in after years, and became critical in grammar, though I may have forgotten much of it in my old age. I have stated above the sum total of the education with which I opened my public life. Grammar was not just then within my reach, and much delay in progress was caused by a want of knowing how to proceed to get knowledge. Books were not obtainable, had I known what books I needed. There came a young man from some place further east, and commenced clearing a piece of woodland to make him a home. He brought with him a copy of Murray's Grammar, and I purchased it, and paid for it by three days' hard work at chopping, and those three days' work in time made me rich in grammar. I have that old book still as a relic, and keep it for the good it did.

During this time I kept preaching as well as I could, for there was enough to do, and the circuit preachers were so pressed that they were glad to avail themselves of any help within their reach, whom the people were willing to hear. So I struggled on until the spring of 1823, when I left that wild country, and, as it has proved, left it forever, for I have never been back; and now, finding myself in Michigan, in my eighty-first year, I am not likely to wander back to that far-off and rugged land of my boyhood and youth. My thoughts wander back, and powerful associations seem still to connect me with the home of my youth, and I have an ardent desire to look once more upon that transcendently sublime mountain scenery; but it cannot be: I can only revel in memory of the last sight I had of that scenery when, fifty-eight years ago, I left old Delaware. On foot, with a pack on my back, containing all I owned on earth, I trudged in a northwesterly direction, and when I had reached the last summit that overlooked the scene behind me, I gazed for the last time upon those cloud-covered mountains and those deep ravines and valleys between them. There, on those summits and along their rocky sides and in those valleys at their feet, I had gathered what thoughts I had, and had learned what of life I knew. Farewell, farewell forever! I may never look upon thy grand outline again!

I made my next stand in Plymouth, Chenango County, where I made my home most of the time for nearly two years and a half, during which I preached on the Sabbath a large share of the time, and sometimes filled the appointments of the circuit

preachers. Plymouth was then embraced in Leba-
non Circuit, Genesee Conference. Here I formed an
acquaintance with Miss Mary Miller, the daughter of
Mr. John Miller, and after an acquaintance of a little
over two years Miss Miller became Mrs. Lee. The
bride of my choice was the daughter of a respectable
farmer, and had enjoyed fair school opportunities,
which she had well improved, and had acquired a
good education for those times, and was engaged in
school-teaching. I am not ashamed to say that from
her I received some assistance in the further prosecution of my studies, yet it was not long before I was
the better general scholar, for I pressed on, while circumstances compelled her to devote herself to domes-
tic interests—the kitchen and the nursery—and thus
has she been compelled to spend a long time, for we
have grown old since we were married ; for next July,
1882, will bring the fifty-eighth anniversary of our
wedding. We were married on July 31, 1825, and
late in the following autumn we moved from Plymouth to Conquest, in Cayuga County. The moral
atmosphere not pleasing me in Conquest, we removed to Victory, at the warm invitation of Methodist friends. Victory was the central point on Victory
Circuit, of the Genesee Conference, and there, for the
first time in my life, I found myself surrounded by a
strong Methodist community. Brothers Ayleworth
and Jones were the preachers on the circuit at that
time. They were good men and did what they could

to encourage and assist me. Conference came, and they were removed, and others took their place. It was here in Victory that I organized the first Sunday-school I ever saw. I gathered the children in the school-house, for the church was not yet built, and taught them as well as I knew how. I was for some time the superintendent and only teacher for twenty or thirty children. I believe this was the first Methodist Sunday-school organized in that vicinity. It was in 1826. The subject was just beginning to be agitated, and I had the misfortune to be a little in advance of public opinion, as occurred in regard to other subjects in after years, and I met with opposition from a source from which I had least expected it.

I met with no opposition from the parents of the children, who sustained me, but the second preacher on the charge entered a complaint against me to the presiding elder, the Rev. George Gary. The brother did not pretend that it was sin *per se*, but that it was of too small consequence to justify me in neglecting to preach on the Sabbath. There were places which the circuit preachers could not supply and where my labors would be acceptable and useful, and to neglect such opportunities to teach the children, he insisted, was a wrong. Brother Gary was a good and a wise man, and we both agreed to submit the matter to his judgment. My defense was that, as a local preacher, in the absence of any local preacher's plan, I was at liberty to chose my own field of labor, and violated no rule by devoting my labors to the children. It is enough to say I got my case, and went on with my school.

In 1827 I was recommended by the Quarterly Conference of Victory Circuit to the Genesee Annual Conference, and was received on trial after having preached as a local preacher for about six years. I have always regarded my recommendation in the circumstances one of the highest compliments ever paid me. I was living in the center of the circuit, and was well known, having preached in all the principal appointments. The recommendation was given without my asking for it, and voted in my absence, as I did not attend the quarterly meeting; and it was accompanied by a resolution asking my appointment to the circuit as their next preacher. I was received, but the request for my appointment was disregarded, and I was sent to Malone Circuit, more than two hundred miles to the north-east, of which a more particular account will be given in the next chapter.

CHAPTER V.

The Opening of my Traveling Ministry.

THE Conference at which I was received on trial was held at Wilkesbarre, in Pennsylvania, far to the South, and I lived on the extreme northern border, so no preachers would pass me on their return from Conference to bring me word from Conference if I were rejected, and where appointed if received; and the presiding elder into whose district I fell did not know me, nor where I resided, and consequently could not write to me; so I had to wait, wait, wait. After the lapse of weeks the appointments came in the "Christian Advocate and Journal," which had been published a short time, and, a single copy being taken in my neighborhood, I learned my destiny at last. I was received and appointed to Malone Circuit. As stated in the preceding chapter, the Quarterly Conference requested my appointment to Victory Circuit as their next preacher, but that was overlooked, and I was sent hundreds of miles away.

But where was Malone Circuit, was the next question to settle. I did not know, and I did not readily find any person that could tell me. At last I found a gentleman who told me that Malone was a village, the county town of Franklin County, far to

the north-east, where the surface of the country presented a series of hemlock ridges and spruce swamps,
and this was all the information I could obtain.   Of
course, it was prudent that I should find the circuit
before attempting to move my family to it, and so
I packed my portmanteau, bade my wife farewell
until we should meet again, kissed the little one,
mounted my horse, and was off in search of Malone
Circuit.   I pursued the main north-east road, and
passed out of Cayuga County into Oswego County,
and through it into Jefferson County.   On reaching
the village of Adams I found that Saturday night
had arrived there about the same time, and on inquiry I found a good Methodist family, who received me kindly.

The Rev. W. W. Rundell had been their preacher
the past year, and he was appointed for the year to
come, but had not returned from Conference, so they
had no preaching.   I announced myself as a Methodist preacher, on my way to Malone Circuit.   I did
not tell them I would be very willing to preach for
them in return for my kind entertainment over the
Sabbath, but I thought it; yet I was not invited so to
do.   I was not slow to understand the reason.   They
were a young station, struggling for life under the
very shadow of a large Presbyterian Church; they
knew nothing of me only what they saw, and that I
was but a boy, not more than twenty or twenty-one
years old, and they dared not take the hazard of put-

ting me in the pulpit. They were simply mistaken in regard to my age, but the error did not arise so much from an imperfect judgment on their part, as from my appearance. I had a very young look, and no stranger would have believed me to be more than twenty or twenty-one at most. I did not blame them, but thought the time might come when Methodism would be willing to receive my services in Adams village. Just seven years from that time I was sent for to preach a sermon in defense of their common faith in that great two-story Presbyterian Church, and Methodists and Presbyterians heard me with gladness.

On Monday morning I again mounted my horse, much refreshed, and renewed my search for Malone Circuit. I was told that I would probably find the presiding elder at Watertown, about twelve miles on my way. This was the county seat of Jefferson County. So on I hastened to Watertown, and there I learned that the presiding elder was at Brownville, four miles north, down the Black River. I pushed on to Brownville, and there I found the elder in the person of the Rev. Nathaniel Salsbury, quite a young man, just appointed to the district. He was a tall, well-formed man, with a keen, piercing black eye. which he fixed upon me when I told him who I was, as though he was looking through me to learn what there was in me. He was not a man to be controlled in his judgment altogether by outside appearance,

3

and I think he did not place me quite as low in the grade of preachers as some other men might have done on sight. He received me very kindly, but he could tell me nothing about Malone Circuit, more than that it was still far to the north-east, as he was newly appointed to the district, and had never been in that part of the country. He expressed himself as very glad to see me on my way, and said he should have written to me had he known where to address me, and thereby prevented my suspense and unavoidable delay, and that he thought I had done well to get under way so soon as I had. The slightest encouragement did me good, for my heart was beginning to feel heavy within me. I declined his urgent invitation to stop until after dinner and refresh myself and horse, assuring him neither was in need, and that I was anxious to press forward so as to reach my field of labor before the next Sabbath. He told me he would hold our first quarterly meeting in eight weeks from the following Saturday and Sabbath, and then dismissed me with his "May God bless you!" which put new spirit in me, and I dashed on in a long ride through what was known as the old military road, which was made during the war of 1812, from Sackett's Harbor to Ogdensburgh. I soon passed out of Jefferson County into St. Lawrence County, and on reaching Ogdensburgh I bore a little more to the south, and passed through Canton, the county seat of St. Lawrence County. Thence

I passed through Pottsdam, Stockhoim, and so on until I found myself in Franklin County, of which Malone was the county seat. Still I could hear nothing of Malone Circuit. By and by I inquired of a man by the way-side if he could give me any information in regard to Malone Circuit, or direct me to any of the Methodist preaching places in the vicinity. He replied that he could not, but could direct me to the source of such information. "Go," said he, "four miles on this road, take the road leading north and go two miles, and you will find Judge Pierce, who is a Methodist, and he can tell you all about Malone Circuit." I dashed on with new courage, and even my horse appeared to catch the spirit, and the four miles were soon overcome, and I turned the corner, and the two miles were finished, and I brought up at the door of Judge Pierce. It was with peculiar emotions and a beating heart that I knocked at the door, the first door I had reached on my first circuit, and it was the door of a reputed judge, and, of course, a man of intelligence and standing. I had not been slow to learn that my appearance was against me, and that the first impressions I might make were likely to be unfavorable, but the ordeal must be passed. I knocked, and the judge himself came to the door, and, on my announcing myself as their new preacher, he gave me a hearty shake by the hand and a hearty welcome, and led me into his parlor, and introduced me to the Rev. J. M. Brooks, who had traveled the circuit the previous year, and was re-appointed preacher in charge for the present year, with whom and under whom I was to labor. It was fortunate that we had so opportunely met, and it was a pleasant termination of my long journey. After traveling more than two hundred miles through a strange country I had found Malone Circuit.

CHAPTER VI.

Malone Circuit—Opening Scenes—State of the Church.

REV. BROTHER BROOKS received me cordially and scanned me closely, but was not a man to be critical or very discriminating in his judgment. He was a good, honest man, but only a moderate preacher, and, of course, not the man of enterprise to push the banner of Methodism in the face of its foes, as had to be done in those days to make much progress. We soon had things arranged for the year's campaign. A duplicate plan was made out, he taking one and giving me the other. It was a four-weeks' circuit, and each appointment had preaching once in two weeks, so it was arranged that I should fall back two weeks behind him, and commence work; and in this manner we swept around the circuit once in four weeks, and there being two of us, it gave the people preaching once in two weeks at each appointment; and it was so arranged that we should cross each other's path once in four weeks, and meet for a friendly greeting and consultation. In this way we labored together through the year in perfect harmony.

After passing once round the circuit, arrangements were made for sending for my family, which was accomplished in due time, and I felt myself fully inaugurated as a traveling preacher.

Malone Circuit at this time embraced the whole of Franklin County, with appointments on the east in Clinton County, and also on the west in St. Lawrence County, and some on the north in Lower Canada. On the south was an extensive wilderness. It required thirty sermons to go round the circuit and fill every appointment. This did not make Jack a mere toy, by all play and no work; nor did it make me a dull boy, by all work and no play, for I had to keep myself and nag stepping lively to fill the bill.

In the month of February I had the misfortune to lose my horse. This is worthy of notice, because it resulted in one of those kind interpositions of divine Providence which bring relief when faith is under extreme trial. I reached Fort Covington on Saturday, where I was to preach on Sabbath, but was too sick to think of preaching the next day, and wished to reach home, which was about six miles distant, as soon as possible. Not being able to ride on horseback, the friends instructed a young man to harness my horse into a cutter and drive me home. There having been a thaw and a very extreme cold, the roads were one glare of ice. The young man had failed to secure some part of the harness, which allowed the cutter to glide forward upon the horse's heels, and, starting with a fright, the young man held him too tightly by the bit which pressed the cutter more severely against him, until he threw himself sideways, and broke his leg over the thill. Another horse was harnessed before the cutter, and I was taken home, not only sick in body but greatly troubled in mind. I could not command the funds to purchase another horse, the circuit, I knew, was too poor to give me one, and to prosecute my work on the circuit without a horse was simply impossible. Sick with a high fever, I lay with these troubles rushing through my burning brain, and could see no way of escape, no hope; no light gleamed in upon me from any source, and it appeared, in the feverish wildness of my brain, that my mission was cut short by a sudden stroke of Providence. The reader will bear in mind that sick persons do not always reason soundly, do not see things in their clearest light, nor yet maintain their natural courage in its full force. What now appears to me to have been a little wild and still more weak, and may appear more so to the reader, was then to my fever-excited mind a solemn reality; all appeared lost.

About the fourth day Esquire Parkhurst, from Fort Covington, was announced as wishing to see me. Mr. Parkhurst was a lawyer of high standing, a member of the Presbyterian Church, with whom I had formed a very slight acquaintance. On being introduced he took a seat by my bed-side, and after inquiring after my health, and learning the state of my disease, he inquired, in the most delicate manner, if I possessed the means of purchasing another horse. On being told that I did not, he said, "That troubles you, and if you let it continue to trouble you, it will retard your recovery; dismiss it from your mind, and think about your wide field of labor, and how soon, by God's blessing, you will be at your work again. Do not let the horse trouble you; leave that to your friends until you need the horse, and, I trust, that will be but a few days. Good-morning."

If God had sent his angel to encourage me I could hardly have experienced a more sensible relief. The character of the man, and his very kind and yet frank and earnest manner, assured me that he meant business; and I took his advice, and, dismissing my dark forebodings, I patiently awaited results. Mr. Parkhurst went home and headed a subscription and circulated it among his friends, and then handed it over to leading Methodists in the place, who found no difficulty in obtaining the additional amount necessary; and when I was able to resume my labors, which was in about ten days, I had a horse brought to my door, as good as the one I had lost, and I felt very much like repeating the words of Cowper:

"Ye fearful saints, fresh courage take:
    The clouds ye so much dread
Are big with mercy, and shall break
    In blessings on your head.

"Judge not the Lord by feeble sense,
    But trust him for his grace;
Behind a frowning providence
    He hides a smiling face.

Time moved on as it ever moves, yet then appeared to move slowly, and the year seemed very long; yet it reached a close, as each successive year has since done. To this day, one round on that large circuit appears nearly as long as some full conference years have since done.

In those days young men on trial did not attend the Conference until they were to be admitted into full membership. So, while Mr. Brooks left for Conference, I remained at my work on the circuit. As it was his second year on the charge the rule did not admit of his returning, and he knew he should be sent somewhere else.

It was otherwise with me. I might be returned or sent I knew not where. I made a full round of the circuit before I got any word from Conference. When news came I found myself in charge of the circuit without a colleague. I comforted myself as best I could. If I remained on that hard circuit I was saved the labor and expense of moving, and, on the whole, I made myself believe it was for the best, and was satisfied. As no colleague was sent me from the Conference one had to be obtained, or the work must suffer ; and as the presiding elder had no man for me, with the consent of the Quarterly Conference I engaged a local preacher who resided on the circuit, a Brother Hines. My selection was fully justified by the after career of Brother Hines, as he afterward was received into Conference and labored successfully for a number of years, and then died in the faith and went to heaven. The district was divided, and the Rev. B. G. Paddock was appointed presiding elder of the new district, which gave me a new elder. I wish in this place to bear testimony to the ministerial and Christian character of Brother Paddock. I found him a true friend and a worthy minister in every respect. A friendship sprung up between us which lasted to the day of his death. His friendship was not superficial. When I left the Methodist Episcopal Church on account of slavery, while my old friends —and I had many—became my apparent foes, he never abated in his friendship, and when I finally left Northern New York, in 1864, though he had grown old, on hearing that I was about to depart for Michigan he taxed himself with the travel of miles enough to prove any man's friendship to make us a last visit before we left. " The righteous shall be had in everlasting remembrance." The year passed with only usual incidents of an itinerant life, though an itinerant life was not then what it is now, as will more fully appear in the following chapter. We had some revival during the year, and some additions to the Church. Among the persons converted was a young man who in after years entered the ministry, and I believe is now laboring in California. What his career in the ministry has been I am unable to say, but his conversion was remarkable, and brought to light matters which left no doubt on the minds of saints, sinners, or infidels that the work in his case was genuine and thorough.

It was a year of hard toil and appeared long, but its end was reached; and I passed from my first field of labor, I believe, with the friendship and good wishes of all who were friends of Methodism. It is true they did but little for me by way of material support, but then they were poor, and many made more sacrifice to pay what they did than men do now who pay their tens, fifties, and hundreds. I received one hundred dollars for my services the second year. But they had warm hearts, and but few if any ever forgot the boy preacher, as they all thought me on sight, who served them for the years 1827 and 1828. Those early friends have nearly all gone before me to the land of rest. A gentleman of Malone village, about four years ago, on seeing an article from my pen in the "Northern Christian Advocate," wrote to me to inquire if I was the person who traveled Malone Circuit so many years ago. He said he was then a small boy, but remembered me, as I kept my horse in his father's barn. After speaking of the growth of the place and the Church, he added: "If you should now return to Malone, among the numerous membership of the Church you would not find one who was a member when you preached there."

I left Malone Circuit never to return to that field of labor, or to any part of it, for now there are many pastoral charges within its ancient limits. I once passed through it in one of my antislavery missions, and later I flew through it on the railroad, a thing unthought of when I traveled there. A few years after leaving the circuit I attended a camp-meeting a little south of Malone village, which was attended by good results. During this meeting I witnessed a very extraordinary case, which is worthy of record. A brawling infidel was swaggering about the ground, boasting of his disbelief in the existence of a God. When reproved for his unseemly conduct in such a place he even defied God, and defiantly said, " If there be a God let him speak and convince me." He was told that God had spoken in his word and through nature, and that he refused to see and hear; he was like a man who should stop his ears and shut his eyes, or put them out, and then deny the existence of sound and light. He replied, " Then let God touch me and make me feel his power; if he will knock me down without hands I will believe that he is." A few moments later, as he was passing in front of the preachers' stand, he fell as suddenly as though he had been knocked down with a blacksmith's hammer, and lay helpless for some two or three hours, and finally revived in great agony, from which he professed to obtain relief by the forgiveness of his sins through faith in Christ. Of his after life I cannot speak, as I know nothing of his subsequent history.

CHAPTER VII.

Amusing Anecdotes—Religious Warfare.

IT was remarked in a preceding chapter that I had a very youthful appearance until I was thirty years old. This very boyish look deceived many on first sight, and betrayed some into mortifying mistakes.

In my first round on the circuit I every-where looked upon the faces of strangers ; not a soul did I meet whom I had ever before seen or heard of, and, of course, there were none who knew me. At a number of appointments I could not reach the place before the hour of preaching, and my first introduction was a sermon, and our interchange of recognition came after meeting. All knew they were to hear their new preacher, and yet some were so obtuse as not to recognize him in my person until I rose with open hymn book in hand to begin the service. At one appointment, arriving while the people were collecting, I hitched my horse, and, taking my hymn book and Bible from my portmanteau, I left it on my horse, so that those in the house did not see my insignia of office. I walked into the school-house and seated myself in the only chair, which the preacher usually occupied. A good old sister approached me and kindly whispered in my ear that that was the preacher's chair. I was a little nonplussed for the moment, but rallied and told the good old lady I was weary, having come many miles, and would occupy the chair until the preacher came in, when I would abdicate in his favor. The old lady's movement had been noticed by many or all in the house at the time, some of whom, at least, understood the good sister was sold. There was sharp looking at the old lady a few moments later when I rose and commenced the service by announcing my first hymn, and she looked any thing but satisfaction with herself. The public service ended, and a warm class-meeting led by the preacher was brought to a close; a hearty shaking of hands followed. Among the many greetings the new preacher received, those of the good old lady were not wanting, who came up with more apologies than I could consent to hear; thanking her for the interest she had manifested in the new preacher before she knew him, I assured her that she had only acted the part of a true friend, and shown herself a heroine for the cause.

At Malone another little scene occurred. This was a Sabbath appointment. There was no meeting-house in the place, and the court-house was occupied on Sunday as a church. The Presbyterians occupied it two Sabbaths, the Baptists one, and the Methodists one. The other Sabbath the Methodist preached in an old building known as "the old academy." As the preacher in charge occupied the court-house, I had to preach in the old academy. I preached on Saturday about three miles out of town, and rode in on Sunday morning, and went directly to the place of meeting. There was no desk or platform for the speaker, and I seated myself where it appeared suitable to me. I soon found myself surrounded by persons who appeared anxious about the new preacher.

It was not time to begin the service, and the people were collecting, and all watching anxiously for the arrival of the preacher. An inquiry was commenced around me if any one had seen or heard of the preacher. It was known that he was on the circuit, but no one had seen him or heard of his arrival in the village, and fears began to be expressed. I allowed my eyes occasionally to glance over the collecting congregation, and noted a person in a remote part of the house with his keen, piercing eye fixed upon me, who soon turned upon those that were making inquiries for the preacher around me, as though he would look something into them; but his looks did not take, and they talked on. As no one spoke to me, I did not feel called upon to announce myself as the preacher until it was time to commence the service. At the proper time I rose and gave out a hymn, as usual, and proceeded with the service. There was not a soul present I had ever seen before, and when the service was closed, we had a general introduction and shaking of hands. The individual in the remote part of the house, who tried in vain to look into the minds of his friends around me the fact that the preacher was among them, proved to be an intelligent and worthy local preacher, by the name of Paddock. He became my friend and shared his house with me the second year I traveled the circuit, for we had no parsonages in those days. He told me that he knew I was the preacher the moment I entered the house. In answer to my question, how he knew I was the preacher, he said, "I was looking for the preacher in the person of a stranger, and I knew you were a stranger, for I know all who ever attend our meeting. I had heard the preacher was a young man, and you appeared young enough to fill the bill. Moreover, when you entered you surveyed the room with a glance of your eye, preparatory to selecting your seat, as none but a preacher would do."

My verdant looks troubled me, or troubled others for some years, and once came near costing me a night's sound sleep. At the end of my third year I attended Conference at Utica, and was sent for entertainment during the session to a respectable farmhouse just on the border of the city. Late at night, after all in the house were under the dominion of Morpheus save the good old lady, a brother minister called, on his arrival at the seat of the Conference. Being acquainted in the family, he called rather than to go into the city at so late an hour. The good old lady was in what she thought was a bad plight, as she had not an empty bed. But a bright thought occurred to her. She told the brother her son was in a bed by himself in the *garret*, and there was a boy in one of her beds below whom she would call up and send him up to the garret with her son, and thus make a place for him. The brother inquired if the boy was attending the Conference. She said she believed he was, for he had been sent there to board. "Do you know his name?" he inquired. "I believe some of the other preachers call him Brother Lee," was the old lady's answer. It then flashed upon his mind who the boy was, and with much difficulty he persuaded the good old saint to let him lodge in the garret with her son. The next morning, at the breakfast table, the brother, who had enjoyed a good night's rest in the garret, raised the question of the ages of the company, when it came out that I was four years older than himself and two years older in the ministry. The first information I received of what had transpired the evening before was given me by the apology which the old lady attempted to make on hearing our respective ages. The brother appeared to enjoy the joke at the old lady's expense, and somewhat at my expense, for I felt chagrined for the old lady's sake, who appeared to think the mistake she had made almost an unpardonable one.

No class of persons felt more keenly the mistake of taking me to be a boy than religious opponents, who

4

were brave to attack a supposed defenseless boy, while they would have declined a battle with gray hairs. That was an age of religious controversy and doctrinal preaching, and crimination and recrimination were the order of the times. There were no meeting-houses in the country, not one in the county, when I entered upon Malone Circuit, and only one in process of building. There were but few settled pastors, and the different denominations alternately occupied the school-houses, and largely attended each other's meetings, as there was seldom more than one meeting at the same hour in the same place. The members of the several denominations would report to their preacher what had been said against their doctrine, and a reply would be hurled back, and a constant religious warfare was maintained. It was so to a large extent every-where, but more especially in new regions, where social and religious relations were unsettled, but in the process of being formed.

That part of New York State was settled largely from the States of Vermont and New Hampshire, where at that time Congregationalists and Baptists were more numerous than Methodists, which gave a large preponderance against Methodism in the new settlements. The Congregationalists, on coming into New York, affiliated with the Presbyterians, and were usually the strongest party. The Methodists were the newer and weaker Church, and were most strenuously opposed as dangerous heretics, and had to contend for every inch of ground they took and held. Experienced and able Methodist preachers were not sent to that extreme border; indeed, the men could not be found to supply the work, and such border sections had to accept of such as were left after the older and more important portions of the work were supplied. Methodism had suffered for want of men of ability, experience, and weight of character, to defend her doctrines and usages, and to teach her over-confident assailants to be more cautious in their assaults. The brethren had felt their need, and had been praying to God to send them a man that could stand up in the presence of their opposers. When I made my appearance among them I was taken to be any thing but the man they had been praying for; indeed, I had not yet reached manhood in their estimation; I was only a boy. Now there were giants in that land, experienced ministers of other denominations, who had defied the armies of Methodism, and made free to attack them wherever and whenever they saw an opportunity.

The brethren received me kindly, but could not conceal their anxiety in regard to my success. They informed me of the opposition which I must expect to meet, and cautioned me against one man in particular, who was said to be an experienced and able controversialist, and who had attacked every Methodist preacher who came in his way. I was advised to keep clear of him.

I cannot say that these things did not disturb me,

and arouse something like a war spirit in me, but I thought and felt more than I said. I told them I came with the message of peace and good-will toward all men, and should attack no one, and should give no one an occasion to attack me; but I had come to preach the Gospel as understood by the Methodist Episcopal Church, and if any one saw fit to attack me or my doctrine, I should defend myself to the best of my ability. They could do no less than to approve of my proposed course, yet they clearly feared for the result. Nor do I say their fears were a proof of weakness, for appearances were against them, and were largely supported by their past experience. But they rallied around me for the fight, for they saw more clearly than I did that there must be a fight. It was decided that I should locate my family at a place called Bombay. In a short time the son of Anak against whom I had been especially warned made an appointment to preach of a Wednesday evening. Being unengaged I went to hear him, hoping to be an unnoticed hearer. But some of his friends knew me, and informed him of my presence, and he urged me forward, and having seated me in the little desk, stood outside himself, so as to be able to turn round and preach in my face.

He took for his text Titus iii, 14: "And let ours also learn to maintain good works for necessary uses."

A principal point in his sermon was to show the necessary uses of good works. This he did negatively and affirmatively. Negatively:

"1. Good works are not necessary to make Christians of us. No man can make a Christian of himself by good works. A man must be a Christian before he can perform any good works.

"2. Good works are not necessary to induce God to have mercy upon us. God will not have mercy upon us on account of any works we can perform. The truth is, God must first have mercy upon us, and forgive our sins, and change our hearts, before we can perform one good act acceptable to God."

"But," said the preacher, "you will ask me, 'Can I not pray and can I not go to meeting before I am converted?' I answer, No, not acceptably to God. All your praying and all your going to meeting before God renews your heart will only sink you deeper in hell."

Having preached the above, and much more like it, in my face, in the most impudent manner, he had the audacity to ask me to make any remarks I might feel disposed to offer. To say nothing in such circumstances, after being invited to speak, would be regarded as evidence of cowardice or conscious weakness; and to speak without replying to the assault would be understood as a confession of my inability to reply. There was nothing for me to do but to submit to a defeat without striking a blow, or unsheath my sword and take the hazard of a fight with an acknowledged giant. I was neither studied in the technical theology involved nor in the tactics of debate, and had no plan of battle, but circumstances compelled me to unmask my battery and expose my front, and I did it as audaciously as he had made the assault. It was no time to falter, or even show signs of trepidation, though I felt to tremble in every limb. The friends of both were present, and anxiously waiting the results, and I must show a bold front to the foe. It was raining, and the roads were muddy, yet there was a full house. I rose and remarked, "I deeply sympathize with the unconverted portion of the congregation, who have exposed themselves in coming through rain and mud to be told that your coming will only sink you deeper in hell. As a friend I would advise all who believe the doctrine, if any such there are, to go home and stay there until God comes with his irresistible power and converts you, and then, and not till then, do you pray and come to meeting."

Having delivered this brief speech, I resumed my seat, when the preacher turned to me and said, "I should like to ask the brother a few questions."

I responded that I would answer him any question he might be disposed to ask if I could, and if I could not answer I would say so after I had heard his question.

He asked, "Do you believe a bad fountain can send out sweet water?"

My answer was prompt, "No, sir."

He then asked, "Do you believe a bad tree can bear good fruit?"

"No, sir," was my ready answer.

He then inquired, "Do you believe the human heart is depraved?"

I answered by an emphatic "Yes, sir."

He then summed up as follows:

"If a bad fountain cannot send out sweet water, and if a bad tree cannot bear good fruit, if the human heart is depraved, it must be as a bad fountain and as a bad tree; how, then, can it bring forth any good works acceptable to God?"

It was evident he and his friends were enjoying a fancied triumph, while the faces of my friends wore an expression of doubt and anxiety. It was an anxious moment with them. I rose with much apparent coolness, much more than I really felt, and remarked as follows:

"I suppose I believe in the depravity of the human heart as strongly as my brother does. I believe that men are so depraved through the fall that if they were left wholly without grace, and without divine influence, they would never perform a good act, or even think a good thought acceptable to God; but such is not man's condition. God, having given his Son to redeem sinners, he now moves them by his truth and Spirit to repentance and good works; and when sinners, under this divine influence, pray and go to meeting as a duty, and as a means of seeking God, such acts are not the fruit of the depravity of the heart, but the fruit of God's truth and Spirit working in them, and are acceptable to God as from a repenting sinner."

As I resumed my seat the preacher turned to the congregation and said, " We will be dismissed," and pronounced the benediction.

The first battle was ended, and I had the satisfaction of knowing that I was not vanquished. My friends also took heart. My opponent, however, was not satisfied, as afterward appeared, for he sought an occasion to attack me again at another place. He resided at Fort Covington, where I also preached once in four weeks on the Sabbath. I conducted a prayer-meeting with the brethren in the afternoon at an hour when I had no appointment to preach, and he came into my prayer-meeting and made his assault. It was so ordered that there were present some very respectable persons who did not belong to either Church. This was favorable to me, as it furnished witnesses of the unprovoked assault which he made upon me, and of the result. I had given out a hymn commencing

> " Prayer is appointed to convey
>   The blessings God designs to give :
> Long as they live should Christians pray ;
>   They learn to pray when first they live."

He seized upon the last line as teaching his doctrine, that men cannot pray or perform any good works until they are converted. " They learn to pray when first they live," he insisted, was a confession that they did not know how to pray until they did live; that is, live the new life by a renewal by God's Spirit, and consequently they could not pray acceptably to God before conversion.

This attack was made at the moment I pronounced the meeting closed, and the people all stopped to witness the result. I remarked that I thought the hymn a very good one, and that it was true, as a general principle, that men did not commence a life of prayer before conversion, yet I did not hold myself responsible for every doctrine which ingenuity might extort from each poetic expression. I depended upon my Bible for my theology, and it spake very clearly on the subject. "We read, 'Ask, and it shall be given you; seek, and ye shall find; knock, and it shall be opened unto you.' Your theory would make it read, 'It shall be given you, and then ye shall ask; ye shall find, and then ye shall seek; it shall be opened unto you, and then ye shall knock.'"

He replied, "The text you quote does not relate to sinners in their unrenewed state, but to Christians who ask in order to receive, and seek that they may find the blessings they need; but a sinner cannot ask until he has faith, and then he is a Christian, and can pray."

I rejoined, "I have no doubt Christians may claim the promise of the text, but I think it also includes sinners; it is not restricted to any class, and hence it is said to every man, saint and sinner, 'Ask, and it shall be given you; seek, and ye shall find;' and it is true of sinners: those who ask do obtain, and those who seek do find, while none receive who do not ask, and none find who do not seek. According to your theory, that sinners can do nothing to aid their salvation before God converts them, they are not to blame for not praying, it is not their fault that they are not Christians. How can they be at fault, according to your doctrine, until God comes in his irresistible power and converts them? I am here to tell sinners to repent; you are here, according to your own confession, to tell sinners they cannot repent or pray until God sees fit to change their hearts by his own sovereign act, without any condition or action on their part moving him thereto. I submit it to the candid, which position is most in accordance with the Gospel of Christ, yours or mine?"

He clearly began to feel the embarrassment of his position under my last sally, and sought to extricate himself by seemingly coming back to gospel ground. He answered that,

"Sinners are guilty because God commands them to repent and believe, and they refuse. It is their own fault that they do not obey God. I preach to sinners that they ought to repent and believe in Christ, and that they will be justly damned if they do not."

Unskilled as I was in debate, and though much excited, I saw at a glance where the weakness of his position lay, and assailed it directly by what I have since learned logicians call *argumentum ad hominem.* I replied:

" I know you preach that sinners ought to repent, but you also preach that they never do and never can repent or pray until God does for them what he has not yet done, and what is in no sense conditioned upon any thing they can do. I preach to sinners that they can repent and believe, and you stand up here before these persons and dispute it. I tell sinners they ought to pray, and to begin now; that ' whosoever calleth upon the name of the Lord shall be saved ;' and you confront me and affirm that they cannot call upon the name of the Lord until they are saved. I ask you the question, Can sinners repent, or can they not repent ? That these listeners may understand our respective positions, please give a plain answer, yes or no."

He replied, " They could if they would."

I demanded, " Can they will to repent ?"

He replied, " They would if they could."

Beyond this he would not venture, " They would if they could," and " They could if they would."

When I saw I could not drive him from this con-temptible quibbling, I met it directly by saying, " Sinners can repent, or they cannot; if they cannot, you are wrong when you say they could if they would; and if they can repent, you are wrong when you say they could if they would. To say they could if they would implies that they can repent, and to say they would if they could implies that they cannot repent. Thus you contradict yourself every time you shift from one position to the other; both of your positions cannot be true. The predicament in which you place sinners reminds me of a man who said, 'If I were to bring up another family of children, I would bring them up to do as they have a mind to, for mine are so contrary they will not.'" At this the people laughed, and my assailant started for the door, and was heard to mutter as he went out, " It is easier to laugh at an argument than it is to answer it." The good man never attacked me after this.

The above must suffice for the present on the score of religious warfare, and I will close this protracted chapter by saying that, owing to the force of circumstances, and the want of older and more experienced men, without seeking or desiring it, I soon found myself the standard-bearer and champion of Methodism in all that border section. I knew as well as any one my unfitness for the position, but what could I do? The cause needed a defender, and there appeared no one more available, and friends urged me on. I had three qualifications, zeal, courage, and almighty confidence in the truth of Methodist doctrines; and I accepted the situation and did the best I could. And in the process of defending the truth I soon found it to be bad policy to parry all the blows and give none, and so I drew 'the sword, and threw away the scabbard, and have never been back to pick it up.

When I appeared as the standard-bearer of Methodism, the Universalists, in particular, appeared anxious to test the temper of my steel, and challenge followed challenge ; I accepted each, but gave none. These debates will be noticed in their chronological order. I believe that I have been misunderstood in that I have been regarded and represented by many as belligerent, fond of strife and debate. I have been much engaged in controversy, but I believe it has resulted more from the force of circumstances and an honest love of truth, than from a love of debate. As much as I have been engaged in controversy, I never gave a challenge, and never accepted one except when the proposed question involved some fundamental truth. It will now be admitted that in my frequent and earnest debates on the question of slavery, I was on the right side of the question.

CHAPTER VIII.

My First Attendance at Conference—Examination—Opposition and Reception—The Hand of Providence in it—Bishop Roberts—The Conference.

IN those days young men did not attend Conference until they had traveled two years. That probation with me was now ended, and I was eligible to reception into full connection, and must appear and be examined. Conference was to meet at Cazenovia, Madison County, N. Y. This place was only a moderate day's drive from my wife's parents', in Plymouth, Chenango County. As she had not seen them for four years, since I took her from her home, we were very anxious to make them a visit in connection with the Conference. We started with our two children, and had accomplished about sixty miles of our journey of more than two hundred, when my horse took fright and made such a frightful leap as to hurl the carriage upside down so suddenly that one could not realize how it was done. My wife and the youngest child were thrown some distance, and myself and the oldest child were under the carriage. My first discovery was that I was lying upon the ground with a weight upon me, which I attempted in vain to throw off. At this moment the child made an outcry by my side, and it appeared to me

that the end of the axle-tree of the carriage had
pierced her bowels with the whole weight of the
concern, which, if true, would have been fatal. This
state of things nerved me with more than usual
strength, and the carriage upon me became as light
as a puffball, and I extricated myself and child in an
instant. I saw at a glance the child was uninjured,
the axle-tree had struck two inches too low to do the
work of death, and had passed between her limbs.
As quick as thought could act my attention was now
turned to my wife and the other child. The child
was uninjured, but my wife was severely hurt. I
picked up the child and attempted to assist my wife
to rise, which at first she failed to do. At this moment two women from a house opposite, who had
witnessed the catastrophe, came to my assistance.
My wife finally rose with assistance, and was taken
in charge by one of them and helped to the house.
The other took the child from my arms, and then,
for the first time, I turned my attention to my horse,
for up to this time not a single thought had occurred
to me concerning him. He was a powerful and very
spirited animal, and the moment I thought of him
every nerve was startled in a new direction. The carriage was a borrowed one, and my horse was my only
worldly estate essential in my calling. On turning
my attention to my horse I found him lying upon his
back between the thills of the carriage, his feet ex-
tending upward, unable to get a hoof to the ground.

The carriage must have turned over with such force, and the thills taking him in his leap when not a foot was on the ground, just turned him upside down, and left him helpless. Such was his spirit and power, that could he have got his feet under him the carriage would have been torn to pieces, and myself and the child would, probably, have been mangled under it. As it was, the carriage was not materially injured and all escaped unharmed, except my poor wife, who was badly injured. Our journey was at an end ; a passing doctor was soon called in ; a dislocated knee-pan was set right, and all was done that skill could accomplish ; and after a few days I was able to remove her back to Canton, where she could be cared for in a kind family while I attended Conference. The disappointment was very great, especially to my wife, who had anticipated great joy in visiting her father's house after an absence of four years, during which she had dwelt among strangers. The hour seemed dark : one of the darkest clouds hung over us that ever shrouded the providence of God. There was not only the disappointment, but the severe injury which my wife had received ; and then it appeared necessary I should attend the Conference, to do which I must leave her, in her damaged condition, to be cared for among strangers. My presiding elder, Rev. B. G. Paddock, who resided in the vicinity, and whom I had seen by the way, came promptly to my assistance on hearing of my calamity.

He advised me to place my wife and children in the care of a kind family he named—his brother-in-law and wife's sister, by the name of Fish—and to go on to Conference with him, it not being necessary to start under a week, by which time my wife would be much improved. His wise counsel was followed, and the dark dispensation soon began to brighten up, and it proved the turning-point and gave direction to a life-long career. But for that calamity, so dark and oppressive for the hour, these pages would never have been written, I should not have been what I have been, and the world would never have heard of Luther Lee. This has ever been perfectly plain to myself, and I will now, for the first time, explain it to others.

I had come from within the bounds of the New York Conference, and had but very limited acquaintance outside of Victory Circuit, from which I had been recommended. The Genesee Conference had been divided, and I was on my way to the first session of the Oneida Conference; and I was almost entirely unknown to the members of the new Conference, within the bounds of which I had fallen by the division. Also I had been laboring for two years on an extreme border charge, far removed from neighbors, and had not been visited or made a visit to any other charge during my two years on trial. On my way I met the presiding elder, as stated above, who urged me to delay my journey a week and attend a

5

camp-meeting to be held in Gouverneur, declaring
that he expected to be short of laborers, and that my
services would be greatly needed. He finally tried
to hire me to stop, offering me money for my services, supposing, probably, that as I had been on a
poor charge for two years money might tempt me.
I resisted all persuasion and pressed on. I could
have stopped without much self-denial, but I could
not disappoint my wife, for had I complied I could
not have taken her home until after Conference,
whereas our plan was that she should visit during
Conference. I had not gone more than eight or ten
miles, after leaving the elder, when my journey was
brought to a sudden close by the disaster before described. This threw me back upon the elder's hands
for his camp-meeting. I preached three times during
the meeting, and was listened to by the elder and all
the other preachers present, not one of whom had
ever heard me before. After the meeting we all
journeyed on toward Conference, and on reaching
Lowville, in Lewis County, we found another camp-
meeting in session. This was a large meeting, and a
large number of preachers had reached the place on
their way to Conference. Here I was again called
upon to preach, and, as it afterward appeared, by the
help of God I made a favorable and strong impression on the minds of all the preachers present.

We went on to Conference, and I appeared before
the committee of examination, but could sustain no

examination save on the score of common sense in theology, grammar, and geography. Indeed I had no books for the study of any other branches. The committee reported me deficient, and made a most determined effort to prevent my being received into full connection, and, I have no doubt, would have succeeded if no other members had known me better than they did. As it was, my preaching at the two camp-meetings saved me, for every preacher who had heard me rose up for me with as strong a determination to bring me into Conference as the committee had to keep me out; and the result was I was received by a decisive majority. If it had not been for my misfortune I should not have attended those camp-meetings, and if I had not attended those camp-meetings I should not have been received ; and if I had not been received I should have given up the idea of being a traveling minister and returned to my secular calling. But why would I have given up the idea of being a traveling minister ? The answer is, I should have been in just that state of mind to have done it. I should have been utterly discouraged.

1. I knew my own deficiencies as well as others could and better than the committee who opposed me, and felt their attack as apparently just, though without my fault.

2. I had done the best I could during my two years on Malone Circuit, and had done as well, I believed, as any person would have done in my circumstances.

I had been brave, industrious, and successful in sustaining the interests of the circuit, and had studied my sermons and my grammar, and whatever else I had studied, largely on horseback; and then to have been rejected because I had not learned more would have destroyed my last hope of success.

3. I had labored two years on a very hard circuit faithfully and uncomplainingly, and had received to meet my wants, including all my expenses, only *one hundred and ninety-five dollars*. This was but a poor show for future life, with a growing family on my hands. I do not say my friends who pleaded my case in Conference would not have persuaded me to continue and try again, but I think they would not have succeeded; and I have always believed that the upsetting of my carriage determined my course of life, but for which I should never have been known beyond the circle of an ordinary mechanic.

Received into the Conference by a decisive majority, as I was, the opposition with which I met only served to rouse me to greater exertion, and I determined to roll off the reproach, and before I returned to my border field of labor, from my limited means I purchased a Natural Philosophy, a Rhetoric, Buck's "Theological Dictionary," and a few other useful books, which could not have been obtained in that out-of-the-way place in those early times, and the use I made of them my subsequent record, perhaps, is the best witness.

Bishop Roberts presided at the first session of the Oneida Conference, by whom I was ordained a deacon. The Bishop preached a very moving sermon on Sunday morning, at the conclusion of which the deacons were ordained. The Bishop took for his text 2 Cor. v, 20: "Now then we are embassadors for Christ, as though God did beseech you by us: we pray you in Christ's stead, be ye reconciled to God.' I took no notes, but I remember something of an outline of his sermon through the many stirring and noisy years that have since elapsed. In closing up his appeal he cried out, "God never made me a son of thunder, nor of fire, but he has sometimes made me a man of tears. Gather up here, sinners, that I may weep over you." The Bishop was then an old man, and he never after visited the State of New York. He was not a profound man, but he was a good man, full of zeal, and eloquent of speech. I was young then, and am now older than he then was, yet the impression of his sermon still abides upon my heart.

In the afternoon the venerable Abner Chase preached before the ordination of the elders. He, too, was then an old man, but there was great power in his preaching. I never met him again, as he was a member of the Genesee Conference and passed away before I visited that Conference, as I did in after years.

In those days the Conference sat with closed doors,

and no preacher knew where he was going until the appointments were officially announced by a public reading. Of course, most of the preachers occupied the anxious seat during the last session. I had but little solicitude, as I expected to be sent back into that north country, and I felt sure there was not a harder circuit there than I had traveled for the last two years; so I felt safe.

The end was finally reached, the appointments were read, and undivided attention was given to the announcements made from the now open book of destiny. Last on the list came "Potsdam District, B. G. Paddock, Presiding Elder." "All right," I said to myself, "no change of elder." On went the reading, until I heard, "Waddington, Luther Lee, Albon Smith." My fate stood revealed, and I was all animation to dash away to meet my new responsibilities. I had taken my first lesson at Conference, and thought I had learned something which I could usefully apply.

CHAPTER IX.

Waddington Circuit—A Struggle in reaching it—Opening
Scenes—Incidents—A Successful Year.

HASTENING back to Canton, where I had left
my wife and children, I found my wife so far
recovered as to be able to be removed at once to our
new field. We did not return to Malone, but sent a
team for our few household effects, which, as we
knew we must move, we had put up ready to be
thrown upon the wagon.

I was advised that Lisbon would be the best point
for me to attempt to reach first, and as a camp-meeting had been appointed there, to commence soon
after Conference, my attention would first be needed
there. I was entirely ignorant of the best route, and
was directed by a friend who, as afterward appeared,
knew as little about it as I did. He sent me a few
miles the shortest way, if a way it could be called, but
it was such a way as no man ever wishes to travel but
once. It was so at least in our case. It was an old
military road, made during the war of 1812, and had
not been considered passable by carriages for many
years. It was made originally of round logs, now
rotten, through swamp lands, uninhabited for miles.
My wife, not being fully recovered from her injury,

was too timid to venture to ride behind the horse who
had played her so wild a prank. This difficulty was
soon overcome. Brother Smith, my colleague, was
in our company, and consented to have his steady
horse harnessed before the carriage, and ride my more
spirited one.

Brother Smith was a young man from Malone Circuit, and his father's house had been one of my homes
during the two preceding years I had traveled that
circuit, so that we were ready for co-operation, and it
was agreed that he should accompany me to Lisbon,
and then take the carriage home, which I had borrowed in the neighborhood of his father, as he had to
return home before he entered upon his labors. We
were soon on our way—for there was a way for some
miles—but when we reached the old military road,
through the swamp, we found it exceedingly bad.
The old causeway was rotten and broken up, and
there were clay pits in which horse and carriage
would both founder. It was impossible to get the
carriage through with a person in it. Pushing forward in hope of finding better going, we had soon
passed what was too bad to think of recrossing, and
our only hope was to reach the other end, where we
expected to find solid ground and friends who would
give us shelter. So fearful was the way that my wife
could not remain in the carriage, and in her crippled
and enfeebled condition walking was a fearful tax
upon her power of endurance, while Brother Smith

and myself had all we could do to manage the two
horses and get on with the two children. One such
struggle is enough for a life-time, and we have never
found another equal to it. Had I been alone I could
have endured and slept in the swamp, and renewed
the battle again at dawn, but with my enfeebled wife
and children with me I felt my fortitude heavily
taxed. Yet it would not do for me to falter or show
signs of weakness, and I talked bravely and encouragingly, and pressed forward, for we must get through
and reach our friends on the other side before the
night should spread his mantle over us and stop our
progress. We triumphed, but my wife was unable to
walk for days from the effect of overexertion in her
weakness. My colleague, the Rev. Albon Smith, who
stood by me so bravely and kindly through this struggle, is now residing somewhere in the State of Illinois.
May God reward the kindness of his young heart!

The friends in Lisbon received us kindly, and did
all in their power for our immediate comfort, but
were amazed that any person should have directed us
the way we had come.

I entered at once upon my work with courage and
earnestness. The opposition with which I met at the
Conference now lost all depressing influence upon
me, and left upon my mind only a determination to
wipe out the reproach, if reproach it was, by making
myself a scholar. If I could not be a classical
scholar, with the polish and degrees of a collegiate

course, I could be a practical scholar in fact, for my opposers were not graduates, had never attended a college, and what others had done I could do, and, in the estimation of many at least, I did it.

I found the circuit requiring less travel and preaching than Malone Circuit, yet there was work enough and none too much pay to satisfy the most zealous and self-sacrificing. I remained on the circuit two years, which was all the Discipline then allowed. For my first year's labor I received one hundred and fifty dollars, and the second year I did a little better, yet the amount was less than two hundred dollars.

There had been a camp-meeting appointed to be held in Lisbon soon after Conference. This required my early attention, for the arrangements devolved upon me, as there were no other preachers near enough to advise and assist. I staked out the ground and assisted in clearing it and in erecting the preachers' stand. The day came, neighborhood tents were put up, and others were arriving from a distance, and I was busy giving directions here and there, telling this man where he could erect his tent and that man where he could erect his. The weather was warm, and, like a man of hard work, I had thrown off my coat and was flying about in my shirt sleeves, and being a stranger to all save a few residing in the neighborhood of the ground, none supposed me to be the preacher in charge, but regarded me as some local agent employed to superintend the arrangement of the ground, and thought me very young for that. It had been given out that there would be preaching at three o'clock P. M. The hour approached, and no preachers yet reported their presence upon the ground. The people of the neighborhood gathered to hear the opening sermon, and the friends gathered upon the seats from the tents in expectation. My wife was in a tent, with her little ones, near the stand. The time for preaching had come, and the responsibility was upon me. I rose upon the stand and announced the commencement of the services, and gave out a hymn. A lady in the tent said to my wife, "I hope that boy is not going to undertake to preach. I know he cannot preach by his looks. Do you know who he is?" My wife simply answered that it was Mr. Lee; but who Mr. Lee was the lady knew no better than she did before. While I was proceeding with the preliminary service the oldest child became restless, and to pacify it the mother said, "Be still, and listen; papa is going to preach." It flashed upon the lady's mind that she had been talking to the boy's wife of whom she had spoken so disrespectfully, and she shot from the tent in as great a hurry as she would had it been on fire. After the services were closed several persons whom I had directed and assisted in pitching their tents came to me with apologies, they having no idea of my being the preacher in charge of the circuit. The presiding elder and several other preachers came to my relief in the even-

ing, and we had a very successful meeting, which gave
an impulse to the work on this portion of the circuit,
and the conference year opened with fair promise.

Nothing very important occurred during the year
beyond the ordinary moves and changes common to
those times. I first located my family in Lisbon,
found it on one end of the circuit, and moved to
Waddington, and after a time made a second move to
a preaching-place known as the Grass River appointment. A few incidents occurred which may be
worthy of recording as mere indications of the spirit
of those times, and the condition of things which
preachers had to meet.

In the fearful overturn, already described, by
which my wife was injured, her bonnet was demol-
ished, it being an old straw fabric, and, of course, I
had to purchase her a new one. There was a very
worthy sister in the Church, in Ogdensburgh, a principal town in the county, and not distant from Lisbon, who kept a millinery establishment, and to her
I went and told her I wanted a bonnet for my wife,
one that should be suitable and most economical when
price and durability were taken into the account.
She put me up a nice Leghorn, and charged me five
dollars. Now the point is, a principal Methodist family would not pay one cent that year for my support
because my wife wore so costly a bonnet. It may
lessen surprise at this fact when it is stated that the
pious lady of that family purchased a common calico

dress and made it up wrong side out lest she should be proud of its bright colors.

A winter night's adventure may interest some who have no experience in pioneer life. It was during this year that the following little incident occurred as one of memory's dotting points. It was of a Sunday evening, after having preached three times, and rode several miles, and become very weary. The evening service was at a regular preaching place, where a well-to-do farmer usually entertained the preacher, and did it well. But other families claimed attention, and on this occasion I was pressed to go home with a family where I had often been invited, but had never been. I yielded. There were two feet or more of snow on the ground, and the thermometer was down to thirty-five or forty below zero. I found a family of a dozen persons, largely young men and young women, sons and daughters, and only one room in the house. Of course I maintained an active process of thinking where they stored so many during the night. About ten o'clock I remarked that I was very weary, and would like to retire for the night. In response to my request I soon heard the old tin lantern jingle. Lanterns in those days were made of perforated tin, with no glass about them. The candle in the lantern being lighted, I was told to follow and they would show me the way to bed. I was conducted out into the snow, and some few rods through it to an old shanty. This, doubtless, had been their first temporary residence on moving in until they could build a better and regular log-cabin. Having built their permanent house, this was used as a lodging room for company. There had been no fire in it during the winter, and no one had slept there. It was so open that snow had blown in and lay upon the floor, and there I had to lodge after my hard day's labor, in linen sheets. That was a night of terror. I would have given five dollars for the privilege of sitting up all night by the monstrous fire they kept, but had not courage enough to propose it.

In another place I met with a summer-night's adventure, having ridden fifteen miles and preached three times during a very hot day, I was completely exhausted, and on reaching my stopping-place I was ready to fall asleep in my chair before it was decent to ask the privilege of retiring. I put up with a good family in a double log-house, and had one room assigned me, in which was their spare bed. As soon as I could I asked the privilege of retiring. Every thing looked clean, and there was a clock in the room to tick the night away. I was asleep almost before my head touched the pillow, so overcome was I by the labors of the day, but before my head had pressed it ten minutes I was as far from sleep as I ever was in my life. I lay without once feeling sleepy until the clock struck four, when I arose and took off the outside cover from the bed, and after shaking it, rolled myself into it on the floor, and got a short nap, but did not dare to stay long for fear some of the family might get up and discover me. Of course, after a good breakfast, I went on my way rejoicing, for if I did not rejoice over a good night's rest, I rejoiced that I had escaped without losing all the blood I had in my veins.

The year at last came to a close, and in looking the work over, it was seen that the field was so enlarged that more labor was required than two men could perform, and a third man was appointed on the charge, as will be seen in the opening of the next chapter.

CHAPTER X.

My Second Conference—Bishop Hedding—Reappointed to
Waddington—Some Revivals—Hard Work—The Battle
waxes warmer—A Contest with Universalists—A Successful Year.

THE second Conference I attended was held in
the city of Utica, commencing July 15, 1830.
It was presided over by Bishop Hedding. I had
met the Bishop before, he having visited my charge
when I was on Malone Circuit, and preached once
for me, and heard me preach. He then filled my
ideal of a Bishop. His sermon before the Conference did not contain so much fundamental theology
as some sermons I afterward heard him preach on
other occasions, but it was masterly of its kind. I
think it was the greatest in simplicity of any sermon
I ever heard, and I never have known a preacher
who I believe could excel it in simplicity. The
Bishop's sermon was mainly upon the subject of
ministerial fidelity, and he dwelt largely upon the
duty of pastoral visiting, and enlarged upon the
crime of neglecting the sick, infirm, and aged, who
are no longer able to attend upon public worship,
with a power which I have seldom realized in any
other sermon. It was a lesson to both my head and
heart which I have never forgotten, and I have no

doubt many afflicted ones under my pastoral care have blessed God as the result of that sermon to which I listened at so early a period in my ministry.

This Conference was not distinguished by any thing unusual, unless it was the discussion on the subject of temperance. A proposition was submitted to the Conference to change the General Rule by inserting the word *extreme* before the word *necessity*, so as to make the Rule read as it now does, "Drinking them unless in cases of extreme necessity." Over this proposition we had an earnest battle. The opposition was led by the Rev. Elias Bowen, (the late Dr. Bowen.) The affirmative was led by the late Dr. George Peck. One of the most effective speeches was made by the Rev. Goodwin Stoddard. By a figure of speech he marshaled the parties as two great armies, and described the battle, and really roused the temperance men of the Conference to a high degree of excitement. The vote was taken at the conclusion of this speech, and it was carried by a large majority. The Bishop pronounced the vote, and added, in an emphatic manner, "Now let whisky die an eternal death." This was fifty-one years ago, and still the battle rages.

We finally reached the close of the Conference, and the appointments were read. As I listened I heard, "Waddington, Luther Lee, Albon Smith, and Calvin Danforth."

6

This Brother Danforth was also a young man from Malone Circuit, whose father's house was one of my homes, and a good one it was, too. The son was a good young man of great promise, but, alas! like a flower nipped in the bud, his health failed, and he went South to improve it, and died in the State of Georgia.

We entered upon our work, and found enough to do. Hard work and little pay was the fashion of those days, and our trio on Waddington Circuit were in the height of fashion. We had the usual bickering and sparring with other denominations, of which I stood the brunt. The course of the Presbyterians in Norfolk, where I resided this year, called me out in self-defense, in which I read their articles on foreordination, decrees, and election, and I laid my gloves aside while I handled them. At Massena, a principal appointment, the Baptist minister threw so much water in the faces of our people that I felt called upon to preach upon the subject of baptism, in which I repelled his assaults and charged home boldly upon his strongholds. · On the whole we had a prosperous year. We had one revival worthy of special mention. It occurred at an appointment known as Grass River, about eleven miles from Norfolk. There was a class at this place composed of elderly people, but no religious young people. Our quarterly meeting was held at Norfolk, and the good old leader at Grass River came out with his wagon,

and, having an empty seat, he persuaded a young
lady to accept of it and come with him. She was
about seventeen years old. She was not what would
be called a vicious girl, but was very far from being
religious, and was full of frolic and dance, and was
the actual leader of the young people in such matters.
During the Saturday evening prayer-meeting she got
convicted, and went forward for prayers, and was
converted. Of course there would be a decisive
struggle when she returned and met her associates;
she would capture them, or they would capture her.
She saw and felt it, and nerved herself up for the
trial. She met her young friends kindly, yet boldly,
and with tears in her eyes told them what the Lord
had done for her, and exhorted them to join her in
the service of God. They broke down under her
appeal, and there followed a revival in which some
sixty persons, young and old, were converted and
united with the Church.

During this year I had my first set-to—public ren-
counter—with the Universalists. It occurred on this
wise: A meeting-house was built by the community
in De Peyster, Heuvel Charge, without any denominational distinction. When they came to the dedication, they found that the people did not all think alike.
There were a few Methodists, a few Presbyterians,
some Universalists, and many who were nothing in
particular. The Methodists and Universalists were
the two strongest religious parties. The Presbyteri-

ans, being the smallest party, threw their interest into the hands of the Methodists, and it was agreed by common consent that the house should be dedicated by one Methodist and one Universalist sermon. The Methodists called upon me for their sermon. It was the first dedication sermon I ever preached, and I spent much labor in preparing for it, with no reference, however, to Universalism, for I was not aware of the exact state of things. On arriving upon the ground I learned the facts, and the question was raised, "Who shall preach first?" Both preferred the second chance, and it was finally agreed to settle it by drawing cuts, and I drew for the first sermon. It was agreed between us that we would not go out of our way to attack each other's doctrine, but only preach our own frankly and honestly as the occasion required. I was true to this agreement, for my sermon did not contain a single allusion to Universalists or to Universalism, nor did it bring out the doctrine of endless punishment. My theme was the omnipresence of God as essential to his being an object of universal worship. I was alone, but there were two Universalist ministers present, Mr. Langworthy and Mr. Whelply. Mr. Langworthy did the preaching. His was a written sermon, and he could preach only what his manuscript contained. It led him out of his way to attack the doctrine of endless punishment. This I construed into a breach of contract, and rose and so stated at the close of his sermon, and gave notice that I would review that part of his sermon in the evening. This I had a right to do, as no provision had been made for any service in the house in the evening.

A great excitement was the result, and I had a large congregation. My effort was largely off-hand, but, if this gave it less studied finish, it imparted to it more sharpness and vigor. It was not to be expected that the person who had received the scathing, as I administered it, would be satisfied without at least an attempt to repeat the excoriation upon the administrator. He was upon his feet at the close of my sermon, but found it difficult to get a hearing, for the clamor of some of his own friends tended to defeat him. I had thrown off my effervescence and was very calm, and succeeded, by the help of my friends, in procuring silence; but then it was found to be too late in the evening to do much, and the scene closed with a challenge from the Universalist ministers, and an acceptance on my part, to meet in public debate in four weeks.

As this was my first debate by previous arrangement, it stirred me up to fever heat, and the four weeks were spent in making such preparations as my time and means of research would permit. My main dependence was upon the Scriptures.

We met at the time appointed, and the battle was opened. Brother Smith, my young colleague, accompanied me, but took no part in the debate, and I spoke against two. Each party spoke fifteen minutes alternately. "Will all men be finally holy and happy?" was the question in issue. My opponents had the affirmative, and should have led the debate; but I had to lead, as they would not, but only deal in negatives, and attack my positions, without venturing to lead off in support of their own doctrine. After skirmishing in this way for some time, I led off with a regular chain of arguments in defense of the doctrine of endless punishment, and compelled them to follow me, or leave my arguments unanswered. My course, then, was to spend about five minutes, less or more, of each speech, in answer to what they had said which needed a reply, and then, during the remaining ten minutes, press the direct argument. In this manner I kept them on the defensive under the pressure of my best and most carefully prepared arguments, which they were but poorly prepared to rebut, as they could not anticipate them, it being their first hand-to-hand grapple with Methodist theology. Their attempted replies brought out the extremely absurd and easily overthrown consequences of their doctrine. They denied all punishment after death, and affirmed that a man's virtue or vice in this life has no effect on his condition in another world, and that the most wicked of individuals are immediately holy and happy after death. They denied the doctrine of the atonement made for sinners by Jesus Christ, and denied the doctrine of pardon, and maintained that every sinner suffers all the punishment his sin deserves here, in this life.

It may appear strange that men should avow positions so vulnerable in a public debate, but the fact was, my arguments were so constructed and arranged as to leave them no other mode of defense but to vault these terribly absurd consequences, in attempting to do which they fell through and foundered. The debate continued through two days and evenings, and was closed by mutual consent late the second evening. The community became intensely interested and excited, and there was quite a scene at the close. No vote was taken or decision rendered, and no one called for or wished for any, but parties were free in expressing their opinion. Unfortunately for the comfort of my opponents, some persons present, who had imbibed too freely of the ardent, boldly arranged themselves on their side, and poured their laudations upon them from their thickened tongues. While my friends were taking a private contribution among themselves for my benefit, to meet my expenses and remunerate me for my services, a friend on the other side, stimulated to a state of heroism, pulled off his old overcoat, and tendered it to Mr. Langworthy, saying, "I have no money, Mr. Langworthy, but take this; you shall be welcome to it." This was the climax of ridiculousness, and closed the drama, and every man went to his own home. My first great battle was ended, and, in the estimation of

the community, I had won a great victory. Even the
intelligent Universalists did not hesitate to admit that
I was the better debater. The estimation in which
my efforts were held by the community was shown
in the fact that all except the Universalists, without
distinction of party, united in a petition for me to be
their pastor the next year.

Time rolled on ; months and weeks went by, and
my labors came to a close in Waddington Circuit, and I bade the friends farewell around the
charge, for I knew I could not return. It had been
a hard year's fight and very limited support, but good
had been done, and I had won many friends whom it
was painful to leave, however desirable it was on
many accounts. I received a little less than two hundred dollars, which was the best I had done any year,
and I went to Conference in very good spirits. I
had sustained myself well for two years on my second charge, and had won a reputation which at least
made me an equal in the class of fourteen admitted
at the same time. In two years I had wiped out the
reproach of that report of deficiency which the Committee of Examination made against me when I was
received, and I began to feel that an open field and a
fair fight lay before me—that I had a chance to do
and dare—which I had never before realized, and I
went in to win. If there was one ambition which
moved my heart more than all others it was to be an
able and successful minister of our Lord Jesus Christ,

and to achieve this I was ready to do and dare, to work or study by night or day. I really felt that nothing possible would be too great a sacrifice as the price of success in the ministry of the Gospel of the grace of God. This may account for the progress I made and the reputation I won during the next six years.

CHAPTER XI.

My Third Conference—Ordained an Elder—Appointed to Heuvel—A Successful Year.

THE Conference for 1831 was held in Lowville, in Lewis County, and was presided over by Bishop Soule. The Bishop presided with great dignity, and perhaps with a slight show of pomposity, when compared with Roberts and Hedding, who had preceded him. On Sabbath the weather was very fine, and the meeting was held in a grove near by. The Bishop preached in the morning from Heb. v, 9: " Being made perfect, he became the author of eternal salvation unto all them that obey him." It was a very able sermon, eloquently delivered, yet it might have been thought by some to be bordering on the spread-eagle style. At the conclusion of the sermon the elders were ordained, myself included. I know of but one of that class besides myself now living, namely, the Rev. Miles H. Gaylord, of the Northern New York Conference. There may be others, but I know of none. Brother Gaylord may have departed before this date, 1881.

During this Conference, for the first time, I was called upon to preach on one of the evenings during its sessions. I took for my text Mark iv, 3: " Hearken ; Behold, there went out a sower to sow." The three points in my sermon were the sower, the seed, and the ground upon which it was sown. Of course I was somewhat embarrassed, but as by this time I had, by dint of effort, acquired a large degree of self-control and power of concealing my weaknesses from others, probably no one but myself knew I was embarrassed. I learned that it was thought by all I acquitted myself very respectably.

The only thing which occurred out of the usual order of business during this Conference was the election of delegates to the next General Conference. I learned by this election that religious bodies have their politics ; the election was made to turn on the presiding-elder question. A majority of the Conference, as appeared, was in favor of making presiding elders elective by the Annual Conferences. This party was led by the Rev. George Peck. As he was young and a popular leader, and as I was still younger, I fell in under his wing, and voted what was called the radical ticket. I have been told that Dr. Peck changed his views on the subject in his old age. I thought at the time it meant business, and after Brother Peck returned from the General Conference I inquired of him what was done on the subject, when, to my surprise, he informed me that the subject was not called up. It slept for forty years, and was but recently called up.

At the close of the Conference, before reading the

appointments, Bishop Soule made a very pompous speech to the Conference. He said: "I have traveled very extensively in the North and in the South and in the East and in the West, and have lodged in palaces and in cabins; I have slept on the ground in the wilderness, amid savage tribes, with no shelter but the broad canopy of heaven, from which the stars, as watching eyes, looked down upon me. To preach the Gospel to perishing sinners I have braved the winds and frosts of winter and the scorching heat of summer, and have been in perils on the water and in perils on the land, in perils in the wilderness and in perils in the city full, and in perils among false brethren; but hitherto God has been my helper, and I believe God will protect and sustain all who fearlessly pursue the path of duty, however rugged and perilous it may be."

All this was said, and much more, simply to teach us that we should go to our respective fields of labor cheerfully, and not complain of him for bad appointments, all of which we knew before. At the conclusion of this speech the Bishop read the appointments, and as I listened I heard him read, " Heuvel, Luther Lee." My work had been accomplished on Waddington Circuit, and I was ready and ardent for another campaign.

Heuvel Charge took its name from Heuvel Village, on the Oswegatchie River, six or seven miles above Ogdensburgh; but the strength of the charge, at this time, was in De Peyster, where I had the battle with the Universalists, as described at the conclusion of the preceding chapter. I located my family at De Peyster. The charge was composed of these two appointments.

As this was my late battle-field I needed no introduction, and no persons were in danger of mistaking me for any other person than the preacher they expected.

I occupied the church I had assisted in dedicating without let or hinderance, for there was no other party to claim it. The Universalists could no longer maintain preaching as they did before the dedication. Mr. Langworthy made a few attempts to rally his friends, but failed in every attempt. His defeat had been too overwhelming to enable him to re-inspirit his friends. We were brought together, face to face, once during the year under circumstances worthy of a record.

A young man in the neighborhood, after a downward course of dissipation, ended one of his drunken sprees by hanging himself. Of course, he must have a Christian burial, but who should preach his funeral sermon? His friends were divided by such a decisive difference of opinion as to admit of no compromise that did not meet the desires of both parties, and it was agreed that there should be two sermons, one by Mr. Langworthy, my old opponent, and one by myself. As I knew my personal friends were anx-

ious I should speak on the occasion, I consented.
Mr. Langworthy preached first, and took for his text
Psa. xcvii, 1: "The Lord reigneth; let the earth
rejoice; let the multitude of the isles be glad thereof." He insisted that because God reigns he con-
trols all things and is the efficient cause of every
event that transpires, including human actions. From
these premises the conclusion was reached that the
man who lay a corpse before us had fulfilled his mission, and accomplished his destiny, and reached the
end which all will reach, some through one course
of life and some through another, and that end is
eternal happiness. This doctrine he labored to make
comfortable to the friends of the deceased, telling
them that the will of God was accomplished in the
mode of their friend's death no less than it would
have been had he died of a fever, consumption, or of
old age. He took special pains to point his arrows
at me.

My text was Heb. x, 31: "It is a fearful thing
to fall into the hands of the living God."

I first explained what it is to fall into the hands of
the living God. It must have some specific meaning.
There is a sense in which all men, good and bad, are
always in the hands of God; but this is not what this
text means. It cannot refer to good men, for God is
their friend, and will defend them, and keep them as
the apple of his eye. It can only refer to wicked
men, to their being called to an account before God,

to be judged for their conduct. Every sinner may be said to fall into the hands of the living God when he dies in his sins and passes from this world into the world of retribution. Though the final judgment does not take place at death, yet it is to be regarded as the sinner's arrest, preparatory for judgment, and he may be said then to fall into the hands of God.

I then explained why it is a fearful thing thus to fall into the hands of the living God. It removes us from the blessings of this life. It is the end of our probation, and seals up our account for the final judgment. It closes the doors of salvation, and ends all hope for future improvement. To all this must be-added the terrible punishment threatened, which renders the catastrophe fearful indeed.

I next inquired how it could be that, in view of such facts, a man could precipitate himself, unbidden, into the presence of God? It could only occur from the blinding and hardening influence of sin. A course of dissipation not only perverts the judgment and stupefies the conscience, but destroys all the attractions this world can have to hold us in life.

To all this must be added the influence of false doctrines. Men teach that there is no judgment to come, that there is no hell, and that all men, however wicked they are here, become perfectly happy as soon as they die. It may be doubted whether men in their clear, sober minds ever believe these doctrines, yet under the hardening and blinding influence of a desperate course in sin, and amid the ruins of a life of dissipation gathering thick and dark around them, men may believe them, or think they believe them, and take hold upon them as a spring of action, and make a leap for the realization of their truth. If men really believed these doctrines there would be more suicides than there are. If the doctrine we heard to-day be true—namely, that the soul of the corpse before us has passed from the abused and corrupted body to the fullness of eternal joy—he acted a wise part in hanging himself, and there are many others who would be wise to follow his example. Why should the fallen, the downtrodden, the friendless, the homeless, the sorrowful, and the wretched of earth linger here, when, with the approval of God who reigns, with the small expense of a lead pill, a grain of arsenic, or three feet of rope, they can transport themselves to realms of eternal joy. But these doctrines are not true, and we need no surer proof that men do not believe them than the fact that the wretched consent to live, and that others suffer their wretched friends to live. They all know and feel that " it is a fearful thing to fall into the hands of the living God," and suffer on.

I characterized the application of the text to the occasion as inappropriate and absurd. There are occasions when we are called upon to rejoice and be glad in view of the fact that God reigns, but this is not one of them. An attempt to blend this event with the lofty conception of the text is more than inappropriate, it is ridiculous. Try it and see. " The Lord reigneth," as may be seen in the fact that this man hanged himself. " Let the earth rejoice," for we see the result of God's reign : the man is dead before our eyes! " Let the multitude of the isles be glad thereof," for this man has, by the purpose of his heart and the skill of his hands, choked himself to death! I closed with an appeal to sinners to prepare to meet God.

7

CHAPTER XII.

My Fourth Conference—Re-appointed to Heuvel—My Second Year's Labor—Another Battle with Universalists—The Year's Results summed up.

THE Conference for 1832 was held in Manlius, Onondaga County. Bishop Hedding presided. On Sabbath the meeting was held in a grove. The Rev. B. Waugh, the Book Agent at New York, but afterward Bishop Waugh, was present, and preached on the Sabbath, from Exod. xxxii, 26: "Who is on the Lord's side?" The arrangement of the sermon and the leading thoughts were excellent, but there was too much bluster in his manner to be very dignified or very impressive. It was a very quiet Conference, nothing occurring out of the usual routine of business.

I was returned to Heuvel Circuit, as I expected to be, and went back cheerfully, to renew the struggle for another year. We had no general revival, but a steady increase of numbers and large growth of confidence and religious feeling in the community. There was clearly less open vice, less Sabbath-breaking, and much more church-going. More effort was made at Heuvel this year than had been made before, with considerable success. There were several conversions and some additions to the Church. A camp-meeting was held at this place, in a grove on the border of the village, which resulted in much good. As it was my second year on the charge, and as there was a sufficient supply of ministerial help present, I did not take upon myself to preach much. The charge of the meeting devolved upon me, and I called upon such preachers as I thought best adapted to the hour. The meeting progressed rather encouragingly until Sunday, when a great throng was on the ground, and but little was done during the day. I felt it most oppressively. We had yet an evening service. The floating congregation was withdrawing, and the ground began to look deserted. There would be on the ground in the evening but few, save those who were tented on the ground, and the people living in the village, who came out from their houses to each service. These were the people we wanted most to reach. While I was in deep thought on the subject of the evening meeting, which was to be our last, trying to make up my mind whom I would better call upon to preach the last sermon, the preachers came to me and insisted that I should preach. It was what I had not thought of, but what I could not refuse to do at their united request. I felt strangely. It was my own charge. I had hoped for much from the camp-meeting which I had not yet realized. If the meeting closed without something more being done I could hope for but little during the remainder of the year. The more I thought the more troubled in mind I was. A failure that evening appeared like a final failure with me to secure the salvation of that people. I felt, as I afterward told a brother, as though I was to preach the funeral sermon of the community. The hour drew nigh, the people were gathering, and I nerved myself as best I could for the effort. Another brother conducted the opening service, after which I rose and announced my text, John v, 40: "Ye will not come to me, that ye might have life."

It was not my purpose to make a show of skill at sermonizing, but to arrest attention, and make a bold attempt to stir the heart. I therefore struck the main point in my intended discourse first, by saying, "Christ is willing, able, ready, and waiting to save every one of you just now, and here, at this altar." An altar of prayer had been prepared in front of the stand, to which seekers were invited. I continued, "This 'will not,' of which the text speaks, is all that has heretofore kept you from being saved; and this same 'will not' is all that keeps you from being saved now, this moment. If I can overcome, by the help of God, this 'will not' of yours, and persuade you to come to Christ by coming to this altar of prayer, where he will meet you, we shall have salvation." At this point a strange impulse seized me, and I said what would have frightened me at another time, and what for a moment frightened some of my brethren present. It was most unlike myself to say any thing like it, for I was never impulsive or extravagant in the use of language, or presumptuous in my statements. I added to the above: " My only object is to persuade you to come to this altar. When this altar is full of seekers my object in preaching will be secured and I will close. I can break off anywhere when the object is secured. To save time, then, you would better come at once, that we may have more time to pray; for you will come, and, God being my helper, I shall not close this sermon until I see the altar full! Come, then, without waiting; fill up the altar, and I will stop preaching, and we will come down and meet you there. Who will be the first? Who will lead the way? Let some one start, and others will follow." At this point some one made for the altar, and others did follow, and the altar was filled up, and the preachers rushed down, and there was a praying time, and there were conversions, and the meeting had a glorious termination, and there was quite an addition to the Church.

When the scene was past, and the excitement subsided and left me to sober reflection, I trembled at what appeared so much like presumption. I do not relate it as a thing to be commended; I am entitled to no credit for it. If it was of me, it was presumption; if it was the Spirit of God that moved me to it, there was no presumption in it, and no credit is due me for it; to God all the glory belongs.

During this year I had my greatest and last oral

debate with the Universalists, at Antwerp, Jefferson County, N. Y. This was at that time the strongest hold of Universalism in all that country. They had a brick church standing upon a hill in the village, making a prominent show, and it was the only church in the place, or for many miles. Antwerp Circuit embraced the village, with an appointment in the school-house. The circuit at this time was a poor one, and was under the charge of a Brother Gibbs, my friend, and, I suppose, my admirer, but a number of years my junior in the ministry. This brother got into a discussion in an incidental conversation with a Dr. Rogers, a Universalist and physician in the place. The doctor finally challenged him for a public debate. The doctor said, " We have challenged the Presbyterians and the Baptists, and they dare not meet us, and we now challenge the Methodists." This was more than Brother Gibbs was willing to bear, and he accepted, with the condition that he should not be required to debate himself, but should have the right of bringing whom he would to represent the Methodist side; and a written contract was entered into on the spot, so fearful was Dr. Rogers that he would back out. Brother Gibbs selected me as his champion, and Dr. Rogers made choice of the Rev. Pitt Morse, of Watertown. Mr. Morse was acknowledged by all to be the strongest debater they had in all that country. The time for the debate was fixed at a reasonable distance in the future, and the report of the matter spread over that whole country. Some of the cautious non-combatant Methodists were alarmed, and thought the young man too forward and too venturesome for his years. It was not generally known that I had undertaken it against my own taste, to save a friend, who in a moment of excitement had involved himself in a contract for a discussion. I loved my regular work and my regular studies too well to seek any such digressive amusement. Moreover, such a contest was a heavy tax upon both mind and body. Still the murmuring went on, as I afterward learned, for my charge was on one side of the centers of influence, so that I did not know how the Methodist pulse beat on the subject.

At this time Bishop Hedding passed through that country, and called upon some principal families. On being asked if he did not think Brother Lee was too forward and too venturesome for a man of his years, I was told the Bishop replied, "You need have no fears for Brother Lee on that subject. I have heard it preached upon by our strongest men from the St. Lawrence to the Gulf of Mexico, and at the camp-meeting in Canton, a year ago, Brother Lee preached upon it by the request of the preachers, and he went beyond any thing I ever heard before. He had argument enough to overturn all the Universalism in the world." That settled public opinion in my favor, and a general interest was felt in the coming contest.

The time came, the debate was held in the Universalist church. The question was thus stated : " Will all men be finally holy and happy ? " Each disputant was to speak fifteen minutes alternately. My opponent chose one man and I chose another, and they chose a third, and the three constituted a board of moderators, whose business it was to keep order and hold the disputants to the question. No decision on the main question was to be given. There were present nearly all the Methodist preachers in the vicinity. My opponent was accompanied by one of his ministerial brethren, a Mr. Fuller, from Boonville. The issue was very earnestly contested on both sides, through three days and three evenings, when the debate was closed by mutual consent.

As I wish to give an abstract of my principal arguments and replies, as the subject is being again mooted in these latter days, I will make it the subject of the next chapter, and will close this with a brief summing up of the results of the year, which was the sixth year of my traveling ministry. I had been moderately successful on Heuvel Charge, and my labors each year had been regarded by others as a success, and I had come to be regarded as a success in the ministry. I had risen more in public estimation during the last year than in all the years before. This was not true in actual progress, but only in public estimation, owing to the fact that I came to be known through my public debate, and more still through the press in a written discussion which grew out of the debate. I have no doubt many who had known me in earlier years, and knew the rock from which I had been hewn, and the pit from which I had been dug, were astonished at the reports they heard of me. I may safely affirm that probably none were more astonished than myself at the progress I had made, for none knew so well as I how small was my beginning, and what my advancement had cost me in brain work and physical endurance. I felt myself that I had wiped out the reproach of ignorance poured upon me at the time of my reception into the Conference, only four years before. My zeal, fidelity to truth, and success attracted the attention of the appointing power, and I was sent to one of the best charges in the Conference, a thing I had not asked for or expected.

CHAPTER XIII.

My Debate with the Rev. Pitt Morse—An Epitome of the Discussion—A Resort to the Press—The Consequences.

" WILL all men be finally holy and happy ? " My opponent had the affirmative, and must open the argument. It was his privilege to lead the debate, which would have been to his advantage could he have made such a show of argument as would have held me sternly to the work of replying; but he could not or did not choose to do it, but employed himself in sensational declamation over a Methodist hell. I had spared no pains in preparation, and was ready for this play of my opponent, and took the lead into my own hand by commencing to pay out a chain of logic-linked arguments on the negative in proof that all men will not be finally holy and happy. This compelled him to act on the defensive, or to suffer his citadel to be stormed without resistance. His opportunity to lead the argument was lost, for by my careful preparation my arguments were so condensed that I could advance them in less time than he occupied in replying to them, which enabled me to make brief rejoinders in answer to his replies and still keep in advance with my argument, compelling him to follow in my wake. This annoyed him, and he struggled to recover the lead, but without success.   He resorted to every possible expedient to draw me off from my chain of argument.   With this view he challenged me to settle the argument by a single text.   He would quote one text, and I might quote one, and by these we would settle the question.   This I knew was only a ruse to break up my chain of argument, and I replied that my side was not in such a strait as to rest all upon a single text, that I had many texts yet in reserve which I intended to quote.   If he chose to rest the affirmative upon one text he might bring it forward, and I would give it all proper attention.   Repeating his challenge, and blustering by daring me to accept it, he produced his text, which was Psalm cxlv, 9: "The Lord is good to all: and his tender mercies are over all his works."

Of course I was bound not to allow him to make much out of this attempt to draw me from my chain of argument, and to divert the attention of our hearers from it.   I replied at once by saying that, as he offered to rest the whole argument, on his side, upon this one text, he must regard it as the strongest text in the book; if I, therefore, could show that it did not sustain the affirmative, he must admit that no other text could sustain it, and he must confess his cause lost.   I then replied as follows:

" God is immutable, and has always been good unto all, and his tender mercies have always been over all his works, while sin and misery have reigned and earth has groaned under human guilt and woe for six thousand years. The Lord was good unto all, and his tender mercies were over all his works, when he opened the windows of heaven and poured the waters of destruction upon the world of the ungodly, and when he reigned fire and brimstone upon Sodom and Gomorrah. The Lord is good unto all, and his tender mercies are over all his works now; sin reigns and the world lieth in wickedness, and millions shed scalding tears of anguish. If present goodness and tender mercy do not produce present holiness and happiness it cannot be made to appear that they will produce holiness and happiness in the future; for God's goodness and mercy, in themselves, will never be any more powerful than they are to-day. As God's goodness and mercy did not prevent the introduction of sin and misery, it must be unsafe to rely upon them as an unconditional cure for what they did not prevent."

This disposition of his one all-sufficient text roused him to desperation, and he made a desperate defense. He declared that sin and misery are a part of God's plan, and the means which he employs to secure the final holiness and happiness of all men. Sin and misery are in perfect harmony with God's will, while he by means of them is working out the grand plan to secure the final happiness of all. God designs the sin and the misery, and uses them as means to an end, and will make every sin and every human pang contribute to his own glory and the final happiness of all men.

To this I replied that " the theory is wholly unscriptural. God condemns and denounces sin, and if this theory be true, God condemns and denounces his own plans and measures. God forbids sin, and admonishes and threatens to punish sinners, and if this theory be true, God forbids the execution of his own plans and the adoption of his own means, and threatens to punish men for doing what he wills and causes them to do. God represents sin as a great evil, but if this theory be true, it is one of the greatest blessings, and will swell the tide of eternal joy. God represents sin as of great turpitude, and sinners as very guilty; but if this be true, there can be no such thing as turpitude or guilt, or even sin, or if there is sin God is the sinner. This theory of my opponent encourages sin, by representing it as promotive of man's final and greatest good. Does he believe it? If he does, if he is capable of being any more wicked than he is, he ought to rouse every power, and sin with heart, soul, mind, and strength, as a means of enlarging his eternal inheritance in glory."

This ended his special proposition to rest the argument upon a single text, and the discussion proceeded in the direction I had given it.

To present my arguments in full, as I then elaborated them, would be to swell these pages beyond reasonable limits. The following is a mere brief, such as I was then accustomed to use in debate, depending upon my memory or my extemporizing power for filling out as the case might require:

I. Sin and punishment will exist in the future state.

1. All Universalists hold views which involve the fact of sin and punishment after death. Every class of Universalists insist that all punishment is designed to reform the punished. As it is obvious that punishment fails to reform many in this life, they must admit that it will be continued after death.

2. There are some sins which will not admit of punishment in this life. In all cases where life terminates during the act of sinning, as when a man commits suicide, or when the assassin has his brains blown out in his attempt to commit murder, sin cannot be punished before death, and must be punished after death.

3. If punishment is inflicted and endured during this life, to the full extent of the penalty of God's law, it can never be known what the punishment for sin is, how great an evil, on whom it is inflicted, nor for what purpose, since it often fails to reform men.

4. It does not appear that bad men always suffer more in this life than good men.

5. To affirm that there is no punishment after death is, in fact, to affirm that the consequences of virtue and vice are limited to this life, which removes all hope and fear in regard to the future, and leaves men to seek what enjoyment they can in this life, without

any thought of, or reference to, the future. Of course, persons fully believing this doctrine, if any such there are, will live as they list.

6. The descriptions often given of the punishment of the wicked in the Scriptures clearly prove it to be after death, in many instances at least. Matt. xxii, 13; xxv, 30, 46; Rom. i, 18; ii, 8, 9; 2 Thess. i, 7, 8; Rev. xx, 15; xxi, 8.

7. The Scriptures associate the punishment of the wicked with a place, frequently called hell, and some times the bottomless pit. Psa. ix, 17; lii, 15; Matt. v, 29; x, 28; Mark ix, 47; Luke xii, 5; xv, 22. Hell must be in the future world.

8. The punishment of the wicked and the happiness of the righteous are often so connected in scriptural references to them as to prove them both to transpire at the same time, and in the same world, be it in this or in the world to come. Matt. viii, 11, 12; xiii, 41–43; xxv, 31–46; Luke xiii, 28; John v, 28, 29; 1 Thess. i, 7–10. It will not be denied that the righteous will receive their promised reward in the world to come, and there also will the wicked be punished.

9. The Scriptures teach that the punishment of the wicked will be longer than the whole of this life, and consequently it must transpire after death. The Scriptures uniformly affirm that human life is very short. Job vii, 6; viii, 9; Psa. ciii, 15, 16; James iv, 14; 1 Peter i, 24. The Scriptures affirm that the punishment of the wicked will be very long, eternal,

everlasting, for ever and ever. Mark iii, 29; Matt. xxv, 46; 2 Thess. i, 9; Jude 7; Rev. xx, 10.

10. The Scriptures and reason both teach that men will possess the same moral character in the future state with which they leave this. Prov. xiv, 32; Dan. xii, 2; John v, 28, 29. Reason accords with revelation. The essential elements of sin adhere in the mind and not in the body. Conscience and consciousness are both of the mind and not of the body. All that is essential to a responsible moral agent is of the mind and not of the body. There is nothing in the nature of death to destroy sin.

11. The punishment of sinners is so associated with the punishment of devils as to prove it to belong to a future state. Matt. xxv, 41.

12. The Scriptures teach that there is to be a day of general judgment, when all men will be judged together, at which time the wicked will receive their punishment, which proves it to be after death. Eccl. xii, 14; Matt. xxv, 31–33; Acts xvii, 31; John xii, 48; Rom. xiv, 10; 2 Cor. v, 10; 2 Pet. ii, 9; Jude 6; Rev. xx, 12.

13. The Scriptures associate the punishment of the living wicked of Christ's time with the then dead and even long-departed generations, which proves punishment to transpire in a future state. Matt. x, 14, 15; xi, 23, 24; Luke x, 31, 32.

14. The judgment and punishment of the wicked are connected with the second coming of Christ,

which proves the punishment to be in the future state. This point was proved under the last argument, but to that may be added Acts x, 42; 2 Tim. iv, 1; 1 Pet. iv, 5; Rev. i, 7; xxii, 7, 12.

15. The Scriptures connect the judgment and punishment of sinners with the end of the world. Matt. xii, 40–42; John xii, 48; 2 Pet. iii, 7, 10, 12; Rom. xx, 11, 12.

16. There is in the minds of men what appears to be a universal conviction that there awaits them a future state of retribution. This conviction must be a conclusion from revelation, a deduction of reason, or a conviction wrought within by the Spirit of God.

II. The punishment of the wicked in the future state will be endless, and, therefore, all men will not be finally holy and happy.

1. The Scriptures affirm the endlessness of punishment in the strongest terms which language contains to express that idea, such as eternal, everlasting, forever, for ever and ever. Matt. xviii, 8; xxv, 46; Mark iii, 29; 2 Thess. i, 9; Rev. xiv, 11; xx, 10.

2. The Scriptures speak of the punishment of the wicked, and the salvation of the righteous, in contrast, in such a manner as to prove that those who are not punished all their sins deserve cannot be saved, and, of course, can never be made holy and happy. Those who are saved are not punished, and those who are punished are not saved. Matt. xxv, 46;

8

John iii; Rom. ii, 6–8. Some men will be punished for their sins, and those who are cannot be saved.

3. The Scriptures absolutely deny salvation to specified evil doers and characters. Matt. v, 20; vii, 21; xii, 32; Mark iii, 29; Luke xiv, 24; John iii, 3, 5, 36; 1 Cor. vi, 10; Gal. v, 21; Eph. v, 5.

4. The Scriptures teach that there is a possibility and danger of coming short of salvation, and warn us against it. Matt. vii, 13, 14; Luke xiii, 24; 1 Cor. ix, 27; Heb. iv, 1; xii, 15–17.

5. The Scriptures teach that sinners can and do resist the means which God employs to save them. Sinners resist the force of truth. Isa. liii, 1; Matt. xiii, 58; xxiii, 37; Acts xiii, 46; 2 Tim. iii, 8; Heb. iii, 16; iv, 2. Sinners resist the influence of the Spirit. Isa. lxiii, 10; Acts vii, 51; Eph. iv, 30; 1 Thess. v, 19. Sinners resist the influence of divine mercy. Isa. i, 2; v, 4; Luke xix, 41–44; xxiii, 34–37; John v, 40; Rev. iii, 20. Sinners resist and harden themselves under the influence of divine correction and punishment. Isa. i, 5; ix, 13; Jer. ii, 20; v, 3; Rev. xvi, 9, 11, 21.

6. The Scriptures teach that there will come a time with sinners when it will be too late to seek and find salvation. Prov. i, 24–26; v, 11; Isa. xxxviii, 18; Matt. xxv, 11, 12; Luke xii, 25; 2 Cor. vi, 2; Heb. iii, 13, 15; Rev. xxii, 11, 12.

7. The promises and threatenings found in the Scriptures both imply the fact of endless punish-

ment. Prov. xxix, 1; Matt. v, 8; x, 39; xiii, 47–49; xxvi, 24; Mark viii, 5; Luke ix, 24; John x, 12, 25; James iii, 13; Rev. ii, 10; xxii, 19.

8. The penalty of the divine law is termed death, which is endless in its nature. Death is the negation of life, the absence of all life; hence death, whether of body or soul, is endless in itself. A person once dead would remain dead forever, unless quickened by a creative power. Gen. ii, 17; Ezek. xviii, 20; Rom. vi, 23; viii, 6; James i, 15.

9. The condition of sinners after the judgment will not be that of probationers, but that of condemned criminals in a state of retribution. The decisions of the last day are represented as final, and there is not the slightest allusion to a probation or offers of mercy after the judgment-day.

10. In a state of future retribution there will be no available means of salvation. There will be no Holy Ghost; it will have been grieved away. Gen. vi, 3; Eph. iv, 30; 1 Thess. v, 19. There will be no Gospel to move their hearts and promise them eternal life, and it will be too late to exercise faith in a Gospel sense.

11. The Scriptures represent the punishment of sinners as their end, their last estate, their portion. Psa. xvii, 14; lxxii, 12, 18, 19; Jer. xvii, 11; Matt. xx, 51; Luke xii, 46; 2 Cor. xi, 13, 15; Phil. iii, 18, 19; Heb. vi, 8.

12. The Scriptures teach that salvation is condi-

tional, and what is conditional cannot be certain with finite minds, and may fail. Matt. xix, 16, 17; Mark xvi, 16; John iii, 36; Rev. ii, 10; iii, 5, 12."

In pressing these arguments every text was quoted in full, and applied to the point in issue. My opponent, in attempting to reply, raised many side issues, which were met in my rejoinders. Finally, an hour was agreed upon for closing the debate. Then there rose a question, who should have the closing speech. After some discussion, it was agreed that we would close by shortening the time. Each should speak ten minutes, then each should speak five, then each one minute, and that I should have the last minute. My opponent's last minute was occupied with a quotation from Isa. xxv, 6–8 : " And in this mountain shall the Lord of hosts make unto all people a feast of fat things, a feast of wines on the lees, of fat things full of marrow, of wines on the lees well refined. And he will destroy in this mountain the face of the covering cast over all people, and the veil that is spread over all nations. He will swallow up death in victory, and the Lord God will wipe away tears from off all faces ; and the rebuke of his people shall he take away from off all the earth : for the Lord hath spoken it."

I remarked that the text which had been quoted was but a general description of the triumph and blessings of the Gospel. If it really predicts an age of universal piety and happiness, it does not insure the salvation of such as live and die in sin before the golden age comes. We read, Prov. i, 24–26: "Because I have called, and ye refused; I have stretched out my hand, and no man regarded; but ye have set at nought all my counsel, and would none of my reproof: I also will laugh at your calamity; I will mock when your fear cometh." Luke xiv, 24: "I say unto you, that none of those men which were bidden shall taste of my supper."

The discussion was closed. Forty-eight years have since rolled by and been gathered to the years beyond the flood; my opponent passed away years ago, and but few witnesses of that conflict are now in the land of the living to testify to its results. Sure I am I bore off the reputation of having achieved a decisive victory. Universalist preaching was never again maintained in that house, and, after standing unoccupied for some years, it passed into the hands of the Catholics.

Mr. Morse made such statements through the press concerning the debate as were calculated to make those who knew nothing about it believe he had triumphed gloriously, and, to give countenance to his statements, he challenged me to a further discussion through the press. I accepted at once, but preferred another oral debate, and urged it. I had never used the pen, and, like David, I did not like to trust to an armor I had not tried. Having discussed preliminaries for some time without being able to agree on another oral debate, I yielded, and said: "If you will not meet me in another oral discussion I call upon you to meet me in the columns of 'The Magazine,' according to your challenge and my acceptance." "The Magazine" was the Universalist organ, published in Utica, N. Y. This brought things to a crisis, and the battle opened. I published my articles also in the "Christian Advocate," of New York. I had had no experience as a writer, but I was compelled to try it or lose the laurels I had won in the oral discussion. I soon found I was as good a match for my opponent with the pen as I was in oral debate, and I soon felt at home. I had only got my battery in position and opened fire when "The Magazine" shut me out of its columns. Of this I complained, especially because I had not sought admission into its columns, but had been challenged there by Mr. Morse. I affirmed that I had never challenged Mr. Morse, but that he had challenged me. This complaint they refused to publish, but stated that they had received an article from me, and accused me of lying, in that I denied having challenged Mr. Morse, and, as proof, they quoted from my former article the words, "I call upon you to meet me in the columns of 'The Magazine,'" omitting the last part of the sentence as I wrote it. Over this they exclaimed, "The reader can see how much truth there is in Mr. Lee's assertion that he never challenged Mr. Morse;" whereas, if they had given the whole sentence, it would have read, " I call upon you to meet me in the columns of ' The Magazine,' *according to your challenge and my acceptance.*" I wrote them, complaining of this downright dishonesty in garbling my words, so as to make me appear to say the opposite of what I actually said, but they took no notice of my complaint, and gave me no redress.   This brought the discussion to a final close.   Being thus challenged in the columns of a Universalist paper and shut out before I had half finished my argument, and so misrepresented, after consultation with friends I determined to write a book in refutation of Universalism, which was issued from the press in the spring of 1836, a volume of three hundred pages.   That, I believe, was the first book written in this country against Universalism, covering the whole ground.   It was my first effort at book-making ; and, though it may have been wanting in classic polish, it was highly commended for its forcible arguments, and there are now many living persons who have assured me they derived much benefit from reading it.   It has long since been out of print.

CHAPTER XIV.

My Fifth Conference—Appointed to Lowville and Martinsburgh—A Pleasant Year—An Attack of Fever.

THE Conference for 1833 was held at Cazenovia, where it was held four years before, when I was received into full connection. Bishop Hedding presided. We had a quiet Conference. Several distinguished visitors attended this Conference. Among them was Rev. Wilbur Fisk, D.D., President of Middletown University, and the Rev. Heman Bangs, from the New York Conference. Both of them preached during the Conference. Dr. Fisk preached on the Sabbath. His was a missionary sermon, and was very eloquent. By one single dash of his eloquence he brought a large portion of the Conference upon their feet, and I found myself up among the rest. The process was a very simple one. It was soon after the death of Melville B. Cox, our first missionary to Africa. He spoke of Cox, of his worth, of his departure for Africa, and of his death, until we were all attention. Then he added: "As Brother Cox took leave of me he said, 'If I die you must come over to Africa and write my epitaph.' I asked, 'What shall your epitaph be?' He replied, '*Though a thousand fall yet shall Africa be redeemed!*'" It was said in such a manner that it thrilled the whole Conference—a large number sprang upon their feet. It was that sermon which sent the Rev. Squire Chase to Africa, whose health failed, but who came home to die. He was an intimate friend of mine, and told me that it was under that sermon that he received an impression that he must go as a missionary to Africa, which he could never shake off.

At the time of the session of this Conference I had commenced my written controversy with Mr. Morse, which had been read and had excited much interest and comment. On being introduced to Dr. Fisk, as he took my hand he said, " I thank you that you have taken up that controversy against Universalism, and I thank you for having done so well." Many and very flattering allusions were made to the subject, both in and out of the Conference. It was obvious that I had given complete satisfaction to the best thinkers among Methodist preachers, who regarded my arguments as unanswerable. The fact that I was discussing the subject with so much skill was, doubtless, the reason why I was unjustly shut out of the Universalist paper, which occurred soon after this Conference.

I must relate one unpleasant fact which occurred at this Conference in relation to my appointment. Up to this time I had been laboring on the northern border, which was then regarded as a hard section of the Conference, and it was plain that I had only to say the word to come out of that part of the work. Brother Dempster came to me and inquired if he could do any thing for me, which I suppose meant, "Is there any appointment in my district which you would like?" I thanked him, but made no request. The Rev. Josiah Keyes was then on the Black River District, with whom I was intimately acquainted, he having been stationed at Potsdam the first year I was on Waddington Circuit. We were great friends. He came to me and told me he would give me any appointment in his district. He had been stationed at Lowville before going upon the district, and he had some little trouble, and it was thought the Church was a little difficult to manage. After considerable conversation I told him I would not name any charge, but accept of any one in his district he saw fit to give me, excepting Lowville; I did not wish to be sent there. My only objection was the fact that he had met with some trouble there, and I had more confidence in him as a manager than I had in myself. Nothing more was said, and I was perfectly surprised, and, indeed, offended, when I was read out at Lowville. It was not the fact that I was appointed there, but the manner in which it was done. Had he told me he wished to send me there, I would have gone cheerfully, or have gone anywhere he desired me to go. But after being offered any charge in the district, and declining to select for myself, to be sent to the only charge I declined without being spoken to,

stung me to the very heart. When I named it to
him, in his own good-natured and peculiar manner
he laughed, and said I was just the man to go there.
But this did not heal the wound that had been made;
it came too late. The same words before the appointment was made would have been sufficient. A
young man by the name of Rufus Stoddard was received on trial and appointed as my colleague, as
Martinsburgh was then attached to Lowville. Lowville was one of the best charges in the Conference, and I spent two of the best years of my life
on it.

Brother Stoddard, my colleague, boarded in my
family during the year. He was a very excellent
young man, and we spent a very happy year together.
But he was among the early smitten flowers. He
passed to another field of labor, his health failed, and
he went home and died, and I was sent for to preach
his funeral sermon in a little less than two years from
the time he left my family. He was truly a blessed
young man.

John Dempster was appointed to the district when
I was sent to Lowville, under whom I spent three
years, two of which I spent in Lowville, and one in
Watertown. He was the best and truest friend I ever
had. He was a good preacher, a faithful administrator, a wise and safe counselor, and a true and sympathizing friend.

We had two good revivals this year, one in Lowville and one in West Martinsburgh, and a fine addition to the Church. But the pleasant and successful year came to a close, and the next Conference met in Auburn.

The Auburn Conference was held in 1834, and was my sixth. Bishop Hedding presided. Nothing occurred worthy of special notice. I preached during the Conference from Rom. v, 17: "For if by one man's offense death reigned by one; much more they which receive abundance of grace and of the gift of righteousness shall reign in life by one, Jesus Christ."

I was returned to Lowville, with Isaac L. Hunt for my colleague. Brother Hunt was a very genial, good fellow, full of good feeling and full of metaphysics, in which he displayed much skill and tact. It was his first year, yet he was somewhat matured in years and judgment, and did well, and we enjoyed a pleasant year together. He is now a superannuate of the Northern New York Conference. I enjoyed another prosperous year on Lowville Charge, with some revival, but not as extensive as the first year. It was during this year that I commenced writing my book in refutation of Universalism. Not to let it interfere with my labors and other studies, I rose every morning at four o'clock, and wrote until called to breakfast. In this way I progressed very rapidly with my manuscript.

We were severely afflicted at the close of this year

with sickness. My next-door neighbor sickened and died. The doctors could not determine what the disease was of which he died. Not many days after his mother was taken sick and also died. Her disease developed symptoms of typhus fever. A girl living in our family watched with the old lady, and took considerable care of her. Just at this time I went to Conference, which met at Oswego this year, 1835, which was my seventh Conference. My family were all well when I left home. On Saturday, at the seat of Conference, I received a letter from my wife, saying that the girl had been taken sick and had died, and that our children, five in number, were all down with the typhus fever, and that some of them were not expected to live. We had no telegraphs in those days nor even railroads in that country. Much time had elapsed since the letter was written, and I was ninety miles from home. My wife was home with her sick children, probably some of them dead, if not already buried, or would be before I could reach home. My horse had been sent into the country to be kept during Conference. On the reception of the letter I at once sent for my horse, and while waiting for him I disposed of what Conference business I had on hand, got my excuse, and was ready to start the moment my horse came. At three o'clock P. M. I jumped into my buggy, and was off with ninety miles between me and my home of sickness and supposed death, and at early dawn next morning I reined up at my own door, having driven eight miles an hour for ninety miles, including stops, so that the actual speed while under way must have been considerably more than eight miles an hour.

I found my family all alive; the fever had turned with all, and the first taken down were beginning to mend slightly, but all were still very low. My wife was worn out with her watching over so many sick ones night and day, and was coming down with the fever. The doctor had urged her for the last twenty-four hours to go to bed, as the fever was upon her; but how could she, with so many sick children so near the gates of death, when a half-hour's neglect might pass them through? People had become alarmed, and it was difficult to obtain watchers and nurses. No sooner did I reach home than my wife gave up, and had a severe turn of the fever. It was, doubtless, worse on account of her having been so long in an atmosphere of the disease, and having so long resisted its attack. I watched over her night and day until the fever turned, when I was taken, as all the rest had been. The doctor urged me to give up and go to bed, insisting it would only aggravate the disease to hold out longer. I roused myself, and said, "Doctor, I will not have the fever." By this time I had heard from Conference, and learned that I was appointed to Watertown, which was twenty-five miles north. It was now Saturday, and I first made the best arrangement I could for the care of my sick wife and

children, and then harnessed my horse and drove
away. I stopped on Rutland Hill, about four miles
from Watertown, with a Brother Weaver, who belonged to Watertown Church. I told them I was on
my way to Watertown, and did not feel well, and
would stop until morning. I did not dare to tell the
whole truth about the cause of my not feeling well;
they, however, could easily see that I was far from
being well. Most families have some favorite remedy for every disease, and so with this good family.
They had in the house a box of Lee's pills, a celebrated pill of those times, made by a Dr. Lee, and
they insisted that I should take a dose on going to bed.
I consented, but such was the condition of my system
that the pills acted with four times their usual power,
and much sooner than usual, so that by morning they
had spent their entire force. I was very feeble, but
did not let the good family know how bad I was. I
told them I could eat no solid food, but would take
a little gruel. My purpose was to drive down to Watertown and preach, if I could stand up to do it,
but I did not feel able to drive my spirited beast into
town. Now this Weaver family were great people
for fine horses, and I had a very beautiful, sprightly
young animal, and the young men admired her much
when they brought her up to the door. I asked them
if they would like to drive her down to church, and
let me take a seat in the family carriage. They were
pleased with the idea, and so was I, for it was a great

relief to me. I found a congregation in the church without a preacher, and I preached to them and dismissed them for the day, and told them I was not feeling well, but would be on hand to commence my labors the next Sabbath. I stayed until Monday morning, and then started for home, which I reached in the afternoon, a well man. To be sure I felt debilitated, but all symptoms of the fever were gone, and I only had to gather up the little strength I had lost, which required but a day or two. It may be said my course was hazardous, or even presumptuous. It may have been so, but that it saved me from typhoid fever there can be no doubt. There were three things which contributed to throw off the fever, namely, my desperate resolution or will-power; leaving the sick-room and the valley, and going on to Rutland Hill; and the terrible action of the pills I took.

As soon as my wife was strong enough we moved to our new charge. There was not at this time a better appointment than Watertown, and not more than two as good. We enjoyed a very pleasant year on the whole, and had a revival in the winter, and some additions to the Church. During this year I issued my book against Universalism, which was thought at the time by good judges to be an able work. It was a pioneer work, and was timely, and did execution in its day. It is now out of print, as before stated. It is now over forty-five years since it was given to the public. This year, 1836, the Conference sat in Watertown, so that I had the care of it on my own hands. Bishop Waugh presided, who was a new Bishop, and this was a new Conference, it being the first session of the Black River Conference. Nothing occurred at this session which was of general interest. Two facts in regard to myself transpired, which may be worthy of mention.

In consequence of the series of poor-paying charges I had served prior to my last, Lowville, and the great sickness we had suffered, I had fallen behind in my finances. I was square with the world save a debt of about thirty dollars, which was due to the Book Room at New York. The representative present being rather urgent for his due, was overheard pressing me for his claim, whereupon, at the suggestion of Brother Dempster, the Conference put their hands in their pockets and paid my debt.

The other fact was this: Brother Dempster introduced a resolution commendatory of my book against Universalism, and urging the preachers to interest themselves in its sale. This resolution Bishop Waugh refused to entertain, saying the book was a private enterprise, and said that it was improper for the Conference officially to indorse and recommend the sale of any book not issued by the Methodist Episcopal Book Room. Brother Dempster was a very modest man, and quietly took his seat, but chose his own occasion to seek redress. He had been my presiding

9

elder for three years, and, of course, had to represent me in Conference. In those days, in the annual examination of character, when a member's name was called he retired, and the elder represented him in his absence, and others made any remarks they had to offer. When my name was called, and I had retired beyond earshot, as I was told—for there are always some leaky persons in such bodies—Brother Dempster rose and pronounced a very remarkable eulogy. He spoke of my energy of character, of my industry and powers of endurance; how I had written and issued a volume of three hundred pages without intrenching, in the slightest degree, upon my ministerial and pastoral duties. "That book is as remarkable as its author; it is a masterly production; it is like himself, and every thing he lays his hand upon bears the stamp of greatness." It will be thought this was extravagance. It may have been so, but if it was it was that peculiar kind of extravagance of which John Dempster was very capable.

CHAPTER XV.

Appointed to Fulton Charge—A very delightful Appointment—Some Antislavery Members—My Antislavery Experience—The Antislavery Battle opened.

FROM the Watertown Conference I was sent to
Fulton. This place is in Oswego County, on the
Oswego River, about twelve miles up the river from
Oswego City, on Lake Ontario. I found it a very
desirable appointment, one of the best in the Conference. Here I spent the happiest year I had yet enjoyed in my itinerant ministry. We had a good revival and important additions to the Church. There
were but two occurrences during the year demanding
special attention.

A young local preacher got into a discussion in a
school-house a few miles out in the country, with a
preacher of the Christian Church, sometimes called
Christ-ians. They are a kind of Unitarian-Baptists.
He called on me to help him, and I agreed to preach
a sermon at the Christian minister, and he agreed to
preach one at me. I preached upon the important
subject of the divinity of Christ, as that was the doctrine in issue. He followed immediately, but was
unable to follow my chain of closely-connected arguments, and got confused in his attempted reply, and
left the subject, and spent the last half of his time in

exhorting sinners to repent and come to Christ. He gave my young brother no more trouble.

Hiram Mattison, since Dr. Mattison, now in heaven, was then a young man, traveling Lysander Circuit, a little west of Fulton. He got into a public discussion with another Christian—*Christ-ian*—minister, who denied the divinity of Christ. After a drawn battle for a day or two, friends came to me and urged me to go out and take hold of the subject in defense of the divinity of Christ. I refused to have any thing to do with it, without the mutual consent of the parties. The proposition being made, it was agreed to, with the proviso that the other side should have the right of bringing forward another man to meet me. A well-known man, Elder Moral, was sent for to confront me, and we met and crossed our swords. After a brief play, I laid down the following premises: Christ is essential divinity, or he is not. If he is essential divinity, the argument is at an end. If he is not essential divinity, what is he? We have a revelation of only three intellectual and moral natures: divine, angelic, and human. If he is really divine, the argument is ended. Is he angelic or human? I demand an answer.

My opponent replied, "He is neither angelic nor human, but all divine; but not the eternal God. He is the Son God, and, of course, has the same nature of the Father, but is not as old. I have a son; he possesses the nature that I do, but he is not as old as I am."

I replied: "You hear my opponent deny the humanity of Christ, and affirm that he is all divine, of the same nature of the Father, only not so old. Waiving all other objection to this theory, I will state but one, which must be fatal. The Son of God died, and as the Father and Son are of the same nature, and as the Son died, so may the Father die, and we have no certain assurance that there will be a God on the throne to-morrow. To-morrow God may be dead."

My opponent made an effort to extricate himself, but failed to do it even to his own satisfaction, and he picked up the books he had brought and started for his home.

I found on Fulton Charge what I had never found on any other charge, namely, members of the Church who were active, working, antislavery men, and in connection with this fact commenced my own antislavery history. My attention had been called to the question, but it had made no very deep impression upon my mind. The American Antislavery Society was organized in 1833, and its organization was followed by fearful mobs in the city of New York. The mob assailed the house of Arthur Tappan, who was president of the Society, and carried his furniture into the street and burned it up. They also committed some outrages upon the colored people. These and other like outrages in other places attracted my attention at the time, but while I condemned mob violence, I did not sympathize with the abolitionists, so-called by their enemies. They chose for themselves the title of antislavery men. The reason why I did not sympathize with them was, I had received all my information concerning them from the sayings and publications of their enemies, who greatly misrepresented them, and called them incendiaries, and other vile names, such as amalgamationists, negro-lovers, etc., and I was ignorant of their real principles, measures, and motives. As they were attacked by the religious press I thought they must be a set of desperate fanatics. Light, however, soon began to be disseminated. The General Conference of 1836, held in Cincinnati, discussed the subject. On the part of slave-holders it was discussed very violently, and they demanded silence on the part of the northern branch of the Church, and called upon the northern members to put their foot upon the abolition viper, and crush it out. How this could be done without discussing the subject was not yet so plain as it might have been, and as it was afterward made by the arbitrary attempts, on the part of the Northern Conferences, to crush antislavery ministers. While the Southern men were so violent in defense of slave-holding in the Church, the Rev. Orange Scott, of the New England Conference, stood up alone on the other side, and made an able argument against slavery, both dignified and calm, without a single gleam of fanaticism from beginning to end. The contrast was very marked.

This Conference, also, by resolution, censured two

of its members for attending an antislavery meeting. It also issued a Pastoral Address to the whole Church, in which it advised all ministers and members to wholly refrain from discussing the slavery question. These facts set me to thinking more earnestly, and I began to feel troubled, though I said nothing which could commit me on either side. I had just emerged from an important doctrinal discussion, and had been absorbed in writing my book, and needed a breathing spell, and time to reflect before I made another plunge into the troubled waters of public discussion, so long as I could avoid it and maintain a good conscience. Yet I will be honest enough to confess that I believe I should have dashed into the discussion sooner than I did had it not been for my very strong Methodist predilections, and that the discussion seemed to me to involve the character and integrity of the Church. I had fought so many battles for her that I was slow to draw my sword against her.

I was now for the first time brought face to face with members of my own Church who were abolitionists, whom I found to be good earnest Christians, who received me and treated me as kindly as the other members, though I made no antislavery profession. Things passed on quietly and the year closed, and I went to Conference with the blessing and prayers of the whole Church that I might be returned to them, and I was returned.

The Conference for 1837 was held in Potsdam, St.

Lawrence County, and was presided over by Bishop Hedding. The Bishop came to us from the Troy Conference, where there had been a severe struggle on the subject of slavery, and where he had delivered an address on the subject to the Conference, the object of which was to allay the abolition excitement, and to reconcile antislavery men to slave-holding in the Church, as it existed in the South. Though no issue had yet been made in the Black River Conference on the subject, there were a few preachers who were understood to be antislavery men, and the Bishop took occasion to repeat his address to us. In this address the Bishop took the ground that slavery, as it existed and was practiced in the Methodist Episcopal Church, was justified by the Golden Rule. His language was, "The right to hold a slave is founded upon this rule, 'All things whatsoever ye would that men should do to you, do you even so to them; for this is the law and the prophets.'" The Conference passed without any antislavery explosion, or any one being driven to show his colors on the subject.

I was appointed a commissioner to transact some business with the Oneida and Genesee Conferences, and was obliged to attend both. The Bishop repeated his address at each of these Conferences, so I listened to the golden-rule argument for the third time, and was cloyed. There was considerable excitement in these Conferences, and each developed a strong antislavery feeling, especially the Genesee Conference. I kept quiet, and attended to the business on which I was sent, and meddled with nothing else.

At the Genesee Conference the delivery of the Bishop's address was followed by a resolution, asking for a copy for publication, with which the Bishop complied.

I roomed during the Conference with Dr. Nathan Bangs, who said to me, "If I were in Bishop Hedding's place, I would not allow that address to be published." I asked him, Why? He answered, "I would not dare to make such a use of my influence; that address, if published, will be understood, all through the South, as a defense of slavery." I said no more, but I thought some thoughts which burned within, and would have burned some others if they had been spoken loud enough to be heard.

A storm seemed gathering, clouds were seen looming up here and there, and heavy thunder muttered in the distance; but we remained calm at Fulton until the death of Mr. Lovejoy, who was shot by a pro-slavery mob in November, 1837. I was stirred, and judged it wrong to remain silent any longer. I preached a sermon on the death of Mr. Lovejoy, in which I condemned all mob violence, vindicated the principles for the utterance of which Mr. Lovejoy had been killed, and condemned slavery as an unmitigated wrong. Having stated my views, I said: "For this declaration I may be denounced as an abolitionist;" and then added, "If this is abolition-

ism, then am I an abolitionist, and I would be glad,
were it possible, to give my abolitionism a thousand
tongues, and write it in letters of flame on the wings
of every wind, to be seen and read of all men."

This discourse produced considerable excitement,
and a copy was asked for, for publication, and it was
immediately given to the public. But, contrary to
what might have been expected, it produced no division in the Church, and I continued to labor on, having the confidence and friendship of both parties.
But it was not so abroad; I was pronounced an abolitionist, and there was at once a coldness manifested
toward me among old friends; some shunned me,
some denounced me. The official organ of the Church,
the "Christian Advocate and Journal," was severe
against all abolitionists and abolition movements, and
I soon found it necessary to defend the principles and
measures of antislavery, as the only consistent method
of defending myself. President Fisk, of Middletown University, published an article on the death of
Mr. Lovejoy, which, if it did not justify the mob, censured the murdered man more than it did the murder-
ers, and threw the responsibility of his death largely
on himself, for having disregarded excited public sentiment. The design of the article was to forestall and
prevent any revulsive influence the outrage might
have in favor of antislavery. It was in startling
contrast with the sermon which I had just preached
and published, insomuch that no one reading both

could fail to see that one or the other must be fearfully in error.

President Fisk soon followed with a series of six articles, in which he labored to show that the doctrines and measures of the abolitionists were revolutionary in their character and tendency, and must, if persisted in, result in a dismemberment of the Church. These articles were an attack upon every abolitionist in the Church, and stigmatized them as schismatics and revolutionists and great sinners—for the sin of their course was forcibly dwelt upon. These articles were published in the official organ of the Church, which would not admit a word in reply. If not counteracted they would necessarily blast the reputation of every abolitionist in the Church, and this was what they were intended to do. I felt that I had a Christian and ministerial reputation, which had cost me too many years of trial, too much hard labor, and too many sacrifices, to have it all swept away with a few dashes of a pen, wielded by one who had been once loud in my praise. I was stirred to the very core of my heart, and I replied with a boldness and power which friend and foe felt and acknowledged. Proslavery men even confessed that the articles of Dr. Fisk were annihilated, and excused the mentor, on the ground that he wrote his articles in great haste, amid the pressure of business, and wrote them too loosely, not expecting such a reviewer.

As no reply could be made in the columns of the

Church organ in which the articles appeared, I used the columns of "Zion's Watchman," an independent Methodist antislavery paper, edited by Le Roy Sunderland. It is not possible to give even an outline of my reply. I did not deny that the persistence of the antislavery men *might* end in a dismemberment of the Church, but insisted that there was no tendency in their principles or measures, in themselves, which would necessarily produce dismemberment, and if such should be the result the fault would be on the part of the opposers of abolition. Any person could see that the proscriptive and oppressive proceedings of the opposers of abolition must tend to produce division if persisted in. I also demonstrated that slavery was a great and God-defaming and humanity-corrupting and crushing evil in the Church, and that purity should not be sacrificed to union; and that if the Church could not be purified from slavery without dismemberment it would be infinitely preferable to being held together by the bonds of human slavery, and being cemented by the blood of enslaved millions. These articles, while they powerfully counteracted the intended results of the articles to which they were a reply, sealed my destiny as a Methodist preacher, as results soon showed.

I followed up my reply to President Fisk with a series of articles on the sinfulness of slavery in all circumstances. The storm gathered thicker and darker, and pro-slavery thunder was heard in every direction, and antislavery men felt that they should have a better understanding with each other and a closer union. A convention was called to assemble in Utica, N. Y., on the second day of May, to be composed of Methodist ministers and laymen. The convention was regarded as a success. A very able address was delivered on the first evening of the convention on the connection of slavery with the Church by the Rev. Orange Scott. On the second evening of the convention I lectured on "The Sinfulness of Slave-holding." Brother Scott was appointed a delegate to the English Wesleyan Conference, and I was appointed delegate to the Canada Wesleyan Conference. My mission to Canada will be noticed hereafter.

Rumors of persecution and proscription were wafted on every breeze; the atmosphere was hazy; the skies were lowering and portentous, and no one knew where the next pro-slavery thunderbolt would strike. It fell in the New York Conference, and it was a twenty-inch bomb, and exploded with great terror, wounded and crippled and killed. The New York trials must be made the subject of another chapter.

CHAPTER XVI.

THE New York Conference for 1838 was held in
New York City in May, after the Utica convention, noticed in the last chapter. Several preachers
were arraigned and tried for their abolitionism, and as
I acted a part in these trials they must have a place
in my narrative, as they had in my life-scenes. The
brethren sent for me to come down and defend them.
It will be remembered that I was stationed at Fulton,
at the extreme northern border of the State, where
the abolition wrath had been less severe than more
central and southern parts, and I was not yet fully
aware of the terrible rancor of the enemies of abolition, and undertook the case of the brethren in New
York in good faith, hoping to be able successfully to
defend them. Vain hope! their destiny was settled
before they were notified that charges would be preferred against them, as I afterward learned. On
reaching the Conference I had not breathed its atmosphere fifteen minutes before I was notified that
all efforts in behalf of the brethren would be unavail-
ing. As Brother C. K. True was the first to be tried,
I frankly told him that I had no hope of successfully

defending him, that the judgment in his case had been made up for two weeks, and nothing could change it. I told him further I could have no motive in defending him only to assert the great principles involved, as I could not get him clear, and I did not wish to stand up before that Conference and assert great principles and have him back out of them as soon as I had asserted them on his behalf. He pledged me that he would stand by the principles and never yield if it cost his standing as a minister, and I went into the trial as his advocate.

The general charge was "contumacy and insubordination." The specifications were:

"1. Violation of his pledge made at the last Conference not to agitate the slavery question.

"2. Aiding in the publication of an antislavery tract.

"3. Attending an antislavery convention at Utica."

No proof was offered, as nothing was denied. The first specification, charging him with violating his pledge, turned on the construction put upon words, and not upon any conduct of the defendant. He denied no word or act laid to his charge, and the trial proceeded simply upon the arguments of the parties. The Rev. Peter P. Sandford, an old and very able minister of the Conference, appeared as prosecuting attorney, and made a masterly argument of the kind, yet much of it was exceedingly fallacious and absurd. As my only object is to give my defense as a part of my own active life, I shall leave the reader to understand the positions of the prosecution from my defense, which will appear plain. I labored under great disadvantages, having the chair and the whole Conference against me, looking daggers at me, and ready to throw every possible difficulty in my way, resorting to the smallest quibbles and technicalities. Indeed, they were determined I should not have a hearing on the subject of slavery. It required nerve to stand up in such circumstances, and I nerved myself for the work as best I could. I knew nothing was to be gained by a modest, diffident manner, and I struck out boldly.

Brother True opened the defense with an argument on the charge of violating his pledge. He insisted that that pledge was not what the prosecution claimed it was, and that if it would admit of the construction they put upon it he did not so understand it. And he argued very ingeniously that the understanding which he had of the pledge at the time alone could determine his responsibility in the premises. He having finished his argument on that point, I took the floor and proceeded as follows:

" Bishop and brethren : I appear before you as the advocate of an accused brother whose innocence I am anxious to maintain, and regret that I can bring to the aid of my argument no personal prestige, having been denied the common civilities in your body usually accorded to members of a sister Conference."

Bishop Hedding, who was in the chair, sprang upon his feet, and said, " I do not know what you mean by saying you have not been treated civilly." I did not give the Bishop time to say more before I replied: " Bishop, I mean just what I say. You, Bishop, in the presence of other Conferences, have taken me by the hand and said, ' It gives me pleasure to introduce to you Brother Lee, of the Black River Conference.' You have not recognized me here, and I have had no introduction to this body." At this sally the people in the gallery cheered me for my boldness. Dr. Bangs jumped up in a great rage and moved that the gallery be cleared. To this some one objected, a little discussion followed, and it was concluded not best to clear the gallery.

I resumed: " The general charge of contumacy and insubordination contains nothing on which any man can be convicted in the absence of all proof, nor do the specifications affirm any thing wrong; the criminality, therefore, if there is any, must be looked for in the arguments of the counsel on the other side, and to them I will direct my attention. On the first specification you have listened to an able defense from Brother True, and I will not detain you with further argument about the construction to be put upon a vaguely-written pledge, but interpose a higher ground of defense than Brother True has claimed for himself. If the pledge was what the prosecution claim for it it was wrong, such a pledge

10

as no man has a right to give, and can have no morally binding force. God commands Brother True, and every other man, to open his mouth for the dumb, and to "remember those in bonds as bound with them;" and if he gave a pledge not to agitate the slavery question he committed a crime; and if he has violated that pledge, as claimed, he has only redeemed himself from his former error. The soundness of this ground of defense depends upon the fact that slavery is wrong and antislavery right, and that it is always right to oppose wrong and to practice what is right. The counsel on the other side has attempted to forestall this argument by laboring to prove that slavery is not wrong in all circumstances, and in particular as it exists in the Methodist Episcopal Church. There may be a difference of opinion in regard to what is the doctrine of the Methodist Episcopal Church on the subject of slavery. The opposing counsel has affirmed that the Methodist Episcopal Church does not, and never did, hold that slavery is a sin *per se*. To save all discussion on doubtful points as to what is the doctrine of the Methodist Episcopal Church, I will plant my argument on the rock of eternal justice and on the God-given and inalienable rights of humanity, by denying that slavery can be right in any circumstances. I am happy to plant the defense of my brother upon this ground, feeling confidence in my ability to maintain it."

At this point the chair called me to order, and said : " You have no right to discuss the general question of slavery ; it is not in the record."

I replied : " I know it is not in the record, but it is in the argument of the counsel on the other side. I must have the right to prove that slavery is wrong, as the counsel on the other side has been allowed to argue that slavery is right, as practiced in the Methodist Episcopal Church."

At this point Dr. Bangs moved that the decision of the chair be sustained, and it was put and carried before I could say another word. It was the most unfair proceeding I ever witnessed in any trial, but I had no redress. Not another word was I allowed to utter against slavery, only as I could sift it in, mixed up with other issues. It was probably intended to confuse me and break me down, no less than to keep out the question of slavery. But I stood firm and rallied, and, dropping my argument against slavery, I seized upon the next point, and proceeded as follows:

" The brother is charged with contumacy and insubordination in having disregarded and violated the advice of the General Conference. This point has been argued with great earnestness, and the argument demands an earnest reply and critical review in justice to my client. The argument is first based upon the advice of the General Conference, which, it has been claimed, has the force of law. The language of the General Conference is as follows :

" 'This subject [slavery and abolition] has been brought before us at the present session, and, by almost a unanimous vote, highly disapproved of; and while we would tenderly sympathize with those of our brethren who, as we believe, have been led astray by this agitating topic, we feel it our imperative duty to express our decided disapprobation of the measures they have pursued to accomplish their ends. . . . These facts constrain us to exhort you to abstain from all abolition movements and associations, and to refrain from patronizing any of their publications. . . . We have come to the solemn conviction that the only safe, scriptural, and prudent way for us, both as ministers and people, to take, is wholly to refrain from this agitating subject.'

" Whatever consideration this may be entitled to as advice, it is only advice, and has not the first element of law, and cannot be tortured into law or be enforced as law upon any person. Advice is counsel or an opinion offered for consideration ; law is a rule of action to be obeyed without question. If advice on one subject can be enforced as law, all advice must be law on the same principle. This no man will allow or submit to.

" There is advice in the Discipline itself. We read in chap. i, sec. 17:

" 'We advise you, as often as possible, to rise at four. From six in the morning till twelve (allowing an hour for breakfast) read, with much prayer, some of our best religious tracts.' * Will you say that this is law, and that every brother who does not read tracts five hours a day is liable to expulsion ?

" But this position of the identity of advice and law has been attempted to be strengthened against the accused by the action of the Conference at its last session. The following is the resolution which has been so earnestly urged :

" '*Resolved*, That this Conference fully concur in the advice of the late General Conference, as expressed in their Pastoral Address.'

" It was the *advice* of the General Conference this Conference concurred in, and as it was advice before they concurred in it, so it was advice and only advice after they had concurred in it. Their concurrence did not make it more than advice. This Conference has no power to change the advice of the General Conference into law.

" The counsel on the other side attempted further to strengthen his argument by an appeal to the twelfth rule of a preacher, which is, ' Act in all things, not according to your own will, but as a son in the Gospel. As such it is your duty to employ your time in the manner which we direct. Above all, if you labor with us in the Lord's vineyard, it is needful that you should do that part of the work which we advise at those times and places which we judge most for his glory.'

* This was then in the Discipline.

" Two remarks will set this matter right:

" 1. The rule relates to our official work as ministers, and not to our private matters or any thing which we may do without interfering with our proper calling as ministers. This is clear from the language of the rule; it speaks of the time and place of our labors, and hence has reference to the appointing power. If it were shown that Brother True has refused to labor at the time and place assigned him by the appointing power, there would be ground of complaint, but it is not charged that he has neglected his work.

" 2. As the rule relates to our work as ministers it cannot forbid or command what does not belong to our ministerial labor; nothing, therefore, can be construed into a violation of the rule which can be done without neglecting the work assigned us by the appointing power.

" The counsel on the other side has labored hard to sustain the charge of contumacy and insubordination by urging that the defendant's conduct is a violation of his ordination vows. There are two vows which every minister takes. When he is ordained a deacon the following vow is taken of him:

" ' Will you reverently obey them to whom the government over you is committed, following with a glad mind and will their godly admonitions ? '

" When a minister is ordained an elder the following vow is taken of him:

" 'Will you reverently obey your chief ministers, unto whom is committed the charge and government over you, following with a glad mind and will their godly admonitions, submitting yourself to their godly judgments ?'

"These pledges constitute not only the stronghold of this prosecution, but the last hold; if it fails here it must fail altogether, and so the opposing counsel appears to have understood it from the time and power he spent upon them. I will not follow the meanderings of his argument, but rely upon a clear and obvious interpretation of those vows which must address itself to every man's common sense and conscience.

"1. There must be some law for the commands and admonitions of our chief ministers to render them binding and to render their disregard a capital offense.

"The promise to obey our chief ministers can mean no more than obedience to their constitutional authority. If it can be extended to one thing for which no constitution or statute law can be produced their power to command must be unlimited, and we are all sold. When I promised to obey my chief ministers it was with the understanding that it comprehended only their constitutional authority, and this only I ever have and still do hold myself bound to obey.

"2. It is their godly admonitions which we have all

promised to follow, and it is their godly judgments to which we have all promised to submit.

"Two things are required to render their admonitions and judgments godly in any proper sense of the vow taken.

"To be godly their admonitions and judgments must relate to those matters and those only in regard to which they have a constitutional right to direct or control our course.

"To admit that we have pledged ourselves to obey one whisper of admonition or judgment beyond their clearly-defined constitutional authority would be to confess that as Methodist ministers we have renounced all our rights as men and Christians, and placed our judgments, wills, and consciences in the keeping of our chief ministers. I declare I have never knowingly done such a thing, and the longer I live the more I see the propriety of not doing it.

"To be godly their admonitions and judgments, even in those matters where the constitution clothes them with authority, must be according to truth and righteousness. Not all the authority of both Church and State can place any human being under obligation to perform one wrong act or release one from the obligation to perform one moral duty. If slavery is a moral wrong, and God requires us to oppose all sin, there can be no advice, admonition, or command which can lay us under the slightest obligation to 'wholly refrain from the agitating subject.' No one can glance at the consequences of denying these positions without being convinced of their truth.

"1. If one thing, which is not matter of law, and which is not of moral obligation in itself, can be rendered binding by the advice or command of a chief minister, then every thing they see fit to advise or command must become binding upon the same principle, and we shall be upon the border of popery, if not quite over the line.

"2. If one thing, which is not forbidden in the word of God, nor in the Discipline, can be made an ecclesiastical offense worthy of expulsion by the advice, admonition, judgment, or command of a chief minister, we have no security for our standing in the Church, and are at the mercy of the will of our chief ministers. If I believed that the ordination vows which I took really mean what has been claimed for them by the prosecuting counsel in this case I would recant them before closing my eyes in sleep to-night.

"Whatever may be the decision of this Conference to-day, let me predict that there is a day coming, and it is not very far off, when it will be no crime to publish antislavery tracts, to attend antislavery conventions, and to denounce slavery in the Church, or in the State, wherever it may be found.*   In conclusion,

* This prediction, though uttered in the face of the strongest northern pro-slavery Conference, and at the darkest hour of the anti-slavery battle in the Church, has been gloriously fulfilled, and he who uttered it has lived, through the mercy of God, to see the triumph.

if this brother must be condemned to an ecclesiastical death for publishing an antislavery tract, for attending an antislavery convention, or for pleading the cause of the enslaved millions of our land, let him die and enjoy a martyr's crown, and let his grave be unknown ; and when antislavery shall have triumphed, when the Church shall be purified from the pollution and guilt of slavery, and its foul blot shall be washed from the folds of the stars and stripes, and the chains of slavery shall be stricken from the millions in bonds, then, and not till then, let his monument be erected, and his epitaph written."

The arguments being closed the Conference soon disposed of the case by convicting Brother True and suspending him from the ministry.

The case of James Floy was called next, and he made his own defense, and an able one it was; but it availed nothing; he was also convicted and suspended. Then the case of David Plumb was called, and resulted in the same way.

These brethren then gave a pledge to the Conference not to agitate the slavery question, and were restored. Plumb would pledge himself only not to agitate the slavery question while he remained a member of the Conference, intending to locate after his suspension was removed. But when he asked for a location the Conference refused to give him one. The Bishop appointed him to Delaware Circuit, he protesting that he could not go to it on account of family circumstances, which was true. It was one of the most remote and hardest circuits in the Conference, on the Delaware River, among the mountains. He did not go to it, and at the next Conference they expelled him for not going to his charge.

At this time, and for some time after, there was some person connected with the Methodist Book Room who had means of knowing the secret counsels, and who reported to some of the antislavery men what to look out for. Who this was I never knew nor cared. I only knew that the information I received came to me through a reliable channel. From this source I learned that a plan was formed to crush out all the leading abolitionists. The work was to begin in the New York Conference; then Dr. Bangs was to go to the New England Conference and prefer charges against Orange Scott and others; then to perform the same work in the Troy, Black River, Oneida, and Genesee Conferences, and the work would be finished in the spring Conferences. Of course I was marked for decapitation in the Black River Conference. These facts I learned while attending the New York trials. To say that this information did not disturb me would be to say I was more than human. I was excited, but it was only for an hour, when, after reflection, I calmed down into a firm resolve, from which nothing could shake me, to stand firm and fight to the last. To be sure, it required nerve and courage, for I was a poor man, with a family of six children, dependent upon my profession for a support.

They had been entirely successful in the New York Conference, but how they would succeed in the other Conferences was doubtful. I could form no certain opinion of the result in my own Conference; we had never had a struggle. I only knew that there was one man who, if he must fall, would fall with armor on, with his face to the foe. I returned home after the trials in New York, and resumed my labors. The time passed rapidly; the New England Conference met, charges were preferred against Orange Scott, and Bishop Hedding appeared as prosecutor, and the power of his influence, eloquence, and tears were exerted to overthrow Brother Scott. The Bishop had become greatly excited over some criticisms on his pro-slavery administration, and he was really extravagant in his efforts to secure the conviction of Scott, but he failed. Scott came out of the trial without even a censure.

Next came the Troy Conference, and the pro-slavery powers were again defeated. They met a spirit and power they did not expect. The onslaught was made upon a brilliant young man, by the name of Spooner, who was arrested on charges growing out of his abolitionism. Those who sympathized with Brother Spooner, exerted themselves to prevent a trial, by quieting and reconciling things, not wishing to come to an open rupture, as they knew would be the case if the trial proceeded; but their efforts were in vain; the pro-slavery bull-dog smelled blood, and blood he was determined to have. This brought a crisis, and the Rev. Cyrus Prindle stepped forward and said: "If you are determined to press this to a trial, I am ready to meet it; it may as well be met now as ever; I stand with the brother, and I shall contest it to the bitter end, and if he falls I pledge you he will not fall alone. Proceed as soon as you please." Brother Prindle was then in his prime; he had for years been one of the leading spirits of the Conference, always mild and unassuming in manner, yet firm and strong. He was roused, and the flash of his eye and the deep intonations of his voice startled the Conference. They paused, the charges were withdrawn, and the brother's character was passed. Another defeat was sustained, and the programme was abandoned, and no foreign prosecutor appeared at the Black River Conference with charges against me.

CHAPTER XVII.

My Mission to the Canada Conference—Its Failure—Newspaper Discussion in regard to it—The Conference—Antislavery Excitement—Charges Preferred against Me and
again Withdrawn—My Location.

IT was stated in a previous chapter that I was appointed by the Utica Antislavery Convention a
delegate to the Canada Wesleyan Conference to represent the sentiments of the antislavery Methodists of
the States. The Conference met in Kingston, in
midsummer, and I attended, but failed to obtain a
hearing as a representative of an antislavery convention. I had an interview with the president, who
was appointed by the English Conference. I found
him a gentleman, and while he assured me that they
all sympathized with me in my antislavery principles,
they could not receive as a delegate to the Conference
any person coming from an unofficial body. Moreover, he stated that there were three other brethren
from the States who assured him that to admit me as
a delegate would give great offense to the Methodist
Episcopal Church, and he thought it not best to disturb the friendly relations between the two bodies.
In all other respects than the failure of my mission
my visit to the Canada Conference was exceedingly
pleasant. I made no report, as there was no body to

report to, the convention that appointed me having gone back into its original elements.

The three brethren from the States were Jesse T. Peck, C. W. Leet, and A. J. Phelps. These brethren forestalled me, and were there for the express purpose of preventing my reception, and they had been there two days when I arrived. It is not probable that I should have been received in my official capacity as a delegate from the Utica Convention had those brethren not been present, yet I am and ever have been willing that they should enjoy all the credit of securing my exclusion.

Brother Peck gave an account of his visit to the Canada Conference in the "Christian Advocate and Journal" of July 13, 1838. His account, among other things, contained the following concerning myself :

Rev. Luther Lee, delegate from the Utica Antislavery Convention, was present during a part of the session, but before any of us arrived. The leading members of the Conference resolved that they could not receive him in that office. The meeting by which he was appointed was considered by the Methodist Episcopal Church as illegitimate and revolutionary in its tendency. The leading measures were deemed by our General Conference and principal men as schismatical and highly dangerous. They could not, therefore, consistently with the friendly relations existing between the great bodies of Methodists, receive their representatives, or extend to them in any sense their official sanction.

I believed the above misrepresented the facts, as I was not there before they arrived, while they were there two days before I arrived. Also in some other points I judged the account unfair, and replied to it in "Zion's Watchman," as I could get no hearing in the "Christian Advocate and Journal." I was a little stung and wrote rather sharply, and some of my remarks may appear somewhat ironical. As my reply was made the basis of charges against me at the Conference, I give the article in full:

"THE CANADA CONFERENCE."

MR. EDITOR: The above is the title of an article published in the 619th number of the " Christian Advocate and Journal," from the pen of Rev. J. T. Peck, which, from the allusion it makes to myself, is entitled to a few moments of my attention.

The first thing I wish to correct is a mistake which I suppose the printer has made—for I cannot suppose that Rev. Prof. Peck would make such a mistake.   The printer then makes Brother Peck say that " Rev. Luther Lee, delegate from the Utica Antislavery Convention, was present during a part of the time, but before any of us arrived." Now, the truth is, I did not arrive at the seat of the Conference until Brother Peck and his associates had been there two days, nor did I leave until some hours after they took their departure.   And I may remark that I should not have left as soon as I did had I not taken a formal leave of the Conference, at the earnest request of Brother Peck, who insisted upon my making an address to the Conference in behalf of all the brethren present from the States, and which, after much urging, I consented to.

Again, Brother Peck says: "The leading members of the Conference resolved that they could not receive him in that office." If by this Brother Peck means, as the language imports, that such a resolution was passed in a conference capacity, or in any other associated capacity, to speak very modestly, I think he is mistaken. If it be so I will be very thankful for a true copy and the resolution, for I have not to this day been informed of any such resolve, nor of any thing like it on the subject. If the leading members of the Canada Conference had any such proceeding, of which I have not been informed, I shall be happy to stand corrected on the receipt of the information. On conversing with some of the leading members of the Conference I was referred to the president, who gave me the following statement of his views. The venerable father said they were with the abolitionists in principle, and that we might rest assured of their sympathies and their prayers, but that he thought it would be improper to receive me in a conference capacity as an antislavery delegate, lest it should disturb the friendly relations between the two bodies. Indeed, this was the principal objection, and about all the one I heard mentioned; and that such an objection should exist was not strange, nor even unexpected to myself. What other state of things could have been expected in view of the course pursued by the "Christian Advocate and Journal," and in view of the fact that Brother Peck was present two days before I arrived, and assured them that if they received me it would most certainly break friendship between the two connections, as he told me he did so assure them ?

As to what Brother Peck says of the antislavery principles of the Canada Conference, I have only to remark that if they embrace the views of President Fisk, Bishop Hedding, and the Rev. N. Bangs, I have very much mistaken the views of the one or the other, for I suppose them to be abolitionists in the common acceptation of the term. If the brethren in Canada think this is a misstatement of their views, I shall take it very kindly if they will correct my mistake, for I do not wish to entertain wrong views of them or of any other class of men.

LUTHER LEE.

FULTON, *July* 20, 1838.

11

That I was not regarded as an intruder and unwelcome by the Canada Conference is certain from the notice which the " Christian Guardian," their organ, gave of my attendance.   After stating that " During the greater part of the proceedings of the late Conference, held at Kingston, several preachers from the United States were present and took part in the proceedings," it added, concerning myself, " Rev. Luther Lee delivered an able and beautiful address on the public admission of the young men into full connection with the Conference.   Mr. Lee forcibly remarked that civil discord had howled like a storm along the border, yet the religious part of the community had no participation in those hostile and lawless proceedings."

The Black River Conference for 1838 held its session in Fulton, so I had the care of providing for it upon my own hands.   It assembled not long after the events described above, and there seemed to be a whispering murmur of trouble in the atmosphere, yet nothing definite was known.   Two Bishops appeared at the Conference—Hedding and Morris.   Morris presided ; but he was a new Bishop, and Bishop Hedding was by his side to support him, if need required. There were present some other brethren from abroad. Conference proceeded quietly until my name was called, when Jesse T. Peck objected to the passage of my character and preferred charges against me. This sent a thrill through the whole Conference and produced great excitement through the entire community, for it spread as on the wings of the wind. I may be permitted to say that I had the respect and confidence of that entire community; even the opposers of abolitionism respected me as a Christian and a minister. The charges were based wholly on my reply to Brother Peck, given on page 160, and hence the reader has the whole of my offending before him. There may have been some facts and circumstances understood at the time which gave point to my article which cannot be fully appreciated now, but all the words are given.

Bishop Morris asked me if I was ready for trial. I replied that I was not; that I wanted until to-morrow morning to prepare my defense, as I had much care on my mind in connection with the Conference, and that I wanted a leisure hour to arrange my defense. The Bishop replied that I could have all the time I desired. "Then," said I, "make it the order of the day for ten o'clock to-morrow forenoon." This was agreed to. My object was secured, which was to have the trial appointed for a definite hour, which would give the community an opportunity to attend, for I knew they would be there. The former custom of sitting with closed doors had now been abandoned, and if any attempt should be made to renew it on this occasion I was determined to resist it to the bitter end, and not submit to a trial other than in public. A silent night hour was devoted to the work of arranging brief notes of the points in my defense, and I went into Conference next morning fully prepared for battle. I was not confident in regard to the result—the Conference had never been brought to a test-vote on the question—nor was this the first thought in my mind. I was becoming a little desperate, feeling that the course the authorities and official organs of the Church were pursuing would, if it had not already done it, cripple or destroy my usefulness as a Methodist minister in the regular work. I intended to make a determined defense of principles and measures rather than of my personal character. As to my accuser, I felt sure I had given him no more occasion of complaint than he had me in the article to which I replied, and my defense was intended to be most terribly severe on him; and, as I was roused—fearfully roused—roused as I was probably never before or since—I have no doubt I should have succeeded in being severe if in nothing else. I have ever since been thankful to God that I was not forced to make that defense.

Ten o'clock came; the seats and gallery were crowded with anxious lookers-on. The case was called, and the Bishop inquired of me if I was ready. My answer was, " Ready." At this point Brother Peck rose, and, with some appropriate remarks in rather a tone of kindness, withdrew the charges, assigning as a reason that he had been pressed and overborne by the leading members of the Conference, who had urged him to this course. He had not changed his mind; he still believed he had just ground of complaint; but he yielded to the earnest persuasion of his brethren, and, as between him and Brother Lee, he would drop the matter, and say no more about it. I responded that I would reciprocate Brother Peck's good feelings, and we would try to be friends. My character was passed, as a matter of course. Still, the fact that charges had been preferred against me in open Conference, and the excitement which had been roused within me, were not so soon disposed of. Thoughts surged in my mind as the ocean waves roll after the wind that raised them has ceased to blow. Meantime I had learned, from a whisperer of secrets, that I was to be sent to Oswego Station. This was true, for the Bishop, who, being a stranger, did not understand the relative desirableness of appointments, told me it had been intended to send me to Oswego. This was in 1838, and the great financial revulsion of 1837 had nearly prostrated Oswego, and the Methodist Episcopal Church in particular, so that it was doubtful if a preacher could be sustained there. This appointment was urged by the presiding elder on the ground that the better charges in the district would not receive me on account of my abolition views. This I knew was incorrect; there were good charges in the district who would have been glad to have received me as their preacher, for my abolitionism had not interfered with my ministerial duties, nor produced a ripple of trouble among the people of my charge. My knowledge of facts left no doubt in my mind that the appointment was intended to punish me for, or to crush out, my abolitionism, and I could not consent to labor under a system of proscription for my opinions, and I asked for and obtained a location.

It was then 1838; it is now 1881. Forty-three years have swept through between the two dates. The two Bishops who were present at that Conference have gone with the years, and most of the members of the Conference have passed away. Among the few that remain is Bishop Peck, who was then my accuser. It is proper to say that the hatchet between us has been buried for long years; and though we met not again until 1878, when I joined him in East Saginaw, at his own telegraphic request, long years since I wrote his name among my personal friends whom I respect and love.

CHAPTER XVIII.

Farewell to Fulton—Engaged as an Antislavery Agent—
The Work Begun—Mobs and Rumors of Mobs—Albany,
West Troy, and Schenectady—Home Again.

IMMEDIATELY after my location, even before the Conference closed, I accepted of an agency for the New York State Antislavery Society, to lecture at large through the State. Some brethren present from the Oneida Conference urged me to come to their Conference, which would meet in a few days, and present my certificate of location, assuring me that I would be received and given a good appointment; but I declined, and entered upon my agency. I could not move before the Sabbath, and the new preacher was on hand, stopping after Conference. Rev. C. W. Leet was my successor, and, being one of the strongest opposers of abolition, I suppose he did not feel quite safe to go home and leave me there among my old friends without watching. He intended to occupy the pulpit all day, but as I had preached no farewell sermon or taken public leave of the congregation and community, my friends were so urgent that Brother Leet yielded, and I was invited to occupy the pulpit for a farewell address. I reviewed my two-years' labor among them, tendered them my thanks for their uniform kindness, for no person had treated me unkindly, and then I gave my reasons for the course I had taken, and justified myself for advocating the cause of the slave. The last part gave great offense to Brother Leet, and he came very near boiling over. That, however, was his business, and not mine. After the Sabbath I commenced preparation for moving. I had resolved to locate my family in Utica, and our means of transportation was a canal boat, which would pass Fulton in the night, and we had to be all ready, with our goods packed and on the dock ready to throw aboard, and ourselves had to be up and waiting. The boats blew a horn on approaching a station. Our last day having come in Fulton, and every thing being ready, we found a shelter and waiting-place until the boat should come in the family of Brother James Whittaker. It would be after midnight, and we had now six children, ranging in age from twelve years to eighteen months.

Brother Whittaker, with whom we spent our last part of a night, was a prominent member of the Church, and one of the most bitter enemies of abolition in the Church; and yet he stood by me to the last, urged me to his house, and when the boat horn sounded, he was up at a bound, and helping to rouse the children, and get them and our hand baggage down to the boat; and after seeing us and all our effects on board the boat, we shook hands, and our intercourse was closed forever. He has been dead for many years, and, I trust, has found a home in heaven.

I had two reasons for locating myself in Utica. The first was, that was the head-quarters of the State Antislavery Society I was to serve; the second was, the Methodist Church there was so thoroughly abolitionized that my standing as a local preacher would be perfectly secure in the Quarterly Conference. No charges for antislavery could be prosecuted against me with success.

My family was soon settled, and I was in the field at my work. To give a detailed account of my labors as an antislavery lecturer is impossible, as it would more than fill my intended volume. I will give a few of the most interesting events which occurred during my efforts in this field of labor. There were already antislavery societies organized in various localities, and where they were not, it was my duty to organize them so far as I could. In Utica there was a Wesleyan antislavery society, which, of course, meant Methodist. At the close of one of my lectures before this society one hundred and thirty names were added to its roll of members.

I soon found that the path of an antislavery lecturer was not a smooth one; opposition gathered on every hand, and violence seemed the order of the day. In many places I got a large and attentive hearing, and in such cases I never failed to convert numbers to my antislavery views. In other places I met with opposition and mob violence, and in such places I converted more to my antislavery views, for mobs appeared more powerful to convict and convince than logic. I visited Cedarville, in Herkimer County. This is the place where it is said the scene is laid of "Ten Nights in a Bar-room." The Methodist Episcopal preacher of this place refused to allow me to occupy his pulpit for an antislavery lecture, and the Universalists offered me the use of their house. The result was, as usual in such cases, the Methodist house was nearly empty at the hour of my lecture.

I lectured at a small place in the vicinity, known as "Smith's Pond." Here I had my first mob. The lecture was in a large stone school-house, the weather was very warm, and the house completely packed with attentive hearers, leaving no room for a mob. Their intention clearly was to have taken me out of the house. They were too late, the whisky was not strong enough, or they did not begin to drink soon enough. Before they got the steam high enough the house was crowded to its utmost capacity, and I was half through my lecture. Then the mob came with a rush. In the neighborhood was a blacksmith of colossal proportions, a man of great physical power. He was an opposer of abolition in an honest way, but had come to hear the lecture, and was standing in the door for want of room and a seat inside. He

was leaning against the door-casing on one side when
the mob came, and so intensely was his attention
given to what I was saying that one or two of the
miscreants passed him before he was aware of it.
But they jostled him, and brought him to a realization of what was going on, and he turned his face to
the crowd without, and stood in the door with his
arm drawn back, saying, "You don't go in there, one
d— scoundrel, unless you go over my dead body."
They dared not attempt to go by him. The few
which passed him rushed toward the stand, not knowing at first that their friends were not coming behind
them. Their attempted dash through the aisle startled some ladies, who shrieked, and roused me to a
sense of what was going on, and I looked the intrud-
ers in the eye, and addressed them as follows:
"Back, you cowardly miscreants! Do you come to
disturb me in the exercise of my right of free
speech! I am the son of a revolutionary soldier,
who fought through seven bloody years to win this
right for me, and do you think I will resign at the
clamor of a mob? No, never! When I do it, let
my right hand forget its cunning; when I do it, let
my tongue cleave to the roof of my mouth; when I
do it, let the ashes of that venerable father awake
from the dead to reprove a recreant son!" This
brought silence in the house; all eyes were turned
on me, and I was about to resume my lecture, when
one of the mob on the outside attempted to come in

at a window. The very thick stone wall caused a very broad window-sill, upon which he mounted, the window being raised high on account of the heat. As large a woman as I ever saw sat opposite the window, who, when her attention was arrested by his attempt to come in past her, rose as calm as one possibly could appear, and seized hold of him and sent him reeling from the sill outward, as though he had been but a kitten. This ended the struggle; the mob was defeated, and I resumed and finished my lecture.

After I resumed my lecture I perceived that some one was burning matches around my feet, and supposed his object was to annoy me with the sulphurous smoke, and paid no attention to his operation. After the lecture was closed and the congregation had been dismissed it was found that he had deposited a quantity of powder about my feet, and had been trying to ignite it with his matches, and had failed, and so I escaped unharmed and unfrightened.

A few evenings later I lectured in the Methodist Church at Crane's Corners, in the town of Litchfield, Herkimer County. Here I was again disturbed. The pulpit was in the front end of the house, and a vestibule in the rear. The weather was very warm, and the door on my left hand as I stood in the pulpit was a little ajar, and the disturbers gathered in the vestibule, and one was heard to say, "Shoot him right in his eyes." In a moment the charge came, and I was saturated with whisky and lampblack from my head down to my chest on my left side. A part of the charge passed me and took effect on the gallery, leaving a black stain that could never be entirely removed. It was done by means of a large gun-barrel, converted into an enormous syringe. I simply remarked that I was not so much prejudiced against color as some persons were, and could talk with a black face, and would finish my lecture, which I did. It took me until midnight to clean myself off.

The next attempt at mobbing me occurred at the village of Remsen, north of Utica. I lectured there of an evening, and, there being rumors of trouble, an overgrown, very stout Welshman, as brave as he was large and stout, volunteered to go with me. He said, "Both friends and foes there know me; friends will stand by me, and foes will not care to come in my way." I had a fair audience, and lectured without much disturbance, only a little grunting and groaning and contradicting, as though there was an element present ready to break out on the first and slightest occasion; yet no stronger demonstration was made, and the lecture was finished, and the congregation dismissed. Then the facts came to light: those groaners in the congregation were waiting for the arrival of their captain with re-enforcements, and he came not. A regular mob had 'been organized; the few there were only the advance skirmishers; the regular line got too drunk to come to time, the leader fell from his horse, and was found and helped home by my brave friend, who was to have defended me if need had required. The devil often overdoes his plans and defeats them. A quantity of whisky is necessary to get up a mob, but too much spoils it.

There was a call for a lecturer in Clinton County, and I was detailed for the service. Clinton is the north-east county in the State, bounded on the north by Lower Canada, and on the east by Lake Champlain. I went through the county and lectured in every town, and almost every school district. I met with less opposition in this county than in any other section of the country. A large majority of the Methodist preachers in the county were abolitionists; those who were not I found free from that bitterness and spite met with almost every-where else. Having accomplished my mission, I returned and reached my home. Meanwhile stern winter had gathered upon the country and wrapped the land in his frosty arms.

After a few days' rest I left home again for Albany, the capital of the State, and lectured for five weeks in the city and vicinity. I found many friends and many bitter opposers. All the Methodist preachers in the city, with one exception, were exceedingly bitter in their opposition to abolitionism. My principal Methodist rallying-point was what was then known as Garrettson Station. I also lectured in Wesley Chapel,

and also in one Presbyterian Church.   I give the following as a specimen of the opposition with which
I met:

The brethren of Garrettson Station desired their
pastor to read a notice of their monthly concert of
prayer for the antislavery cause, which he refused to
do, assigning as a reason that he could not profane the
Sabbath by reading such a notice.   On Sabbath morning there appeared printed notices finely displayed
in conspicuous places in the church.   He declared
that the meeting thus advertised was a disorderly one
and advised the people not to attend it, and said other
sharp things.   This thoroughly advertised the meeting, and the brethren thought it showed a forgetfulness of his Saturday conscience.   The result was more
attended the meeting than ever before.

While lecturing in the city I received a letter of
six closely-written pages, and signed " Clericus," from
which I give the following as specimens:

I defy you to prove from the Bible, except by detached
passages, that slavery is a sin under all circumstances; or to
advance a single precedent from the Bible for the course
which abolitionists pursue in regard to American slavery.

I assert that the bondage of the sons of Ham is in pursuance
of a decree of God; that slavery has existed in all ages of the
world, since the settlement of the progeny of Canaan in the
land called by his name; that slavery is a Bible institution;
that it has never been repealed by divine authority; that we
have no right to interfere with Bible institutions; that we
have only the right to guard the institution of slavery in our
country from abuse.

I had no doubt who "Clericus" was. He was a Methodist preacher then stationed in the city of Albany, in whose pulpit I lectured two evenings during my labors in the city. The trustees opened the house to me, much against his will, and he was much offended at their course, and hurled his spite at me; and we had several unmistakable evidences of his clerical opposition. A gun was fired at the door of the church one evening while I was delivering a lecture. On another evening a stone was hurled through a window during my lecture, but fortunately no person was injured.

I also received the following note, which, if it alarmed some of my friends, did not frighten me. I remembered the adage, "A barking dog never bites." But here is the threat:

ALBANY, *Jan.* 14, 1839.

MR. LUTHER LEE,

SIR:—I would advise you as a friend to leave the city as soon as possible, or you will lose your life. Such conduct as you are pursuing will not do; you must not try to blind people's eyes with false stories. You had not better deliver another lecture in the city; if you do you will surely lose your life. It may not be in the church, but the remedy is sure.

A FRIEND.

Before my return home I visited West Troy, and lectured to full congregations. I found the Methodist preacher in this place exceedingly opposed—so much so that he would not allow me to preach a gospel sermon in his pulpit. As I spent the Sabbath in the place a number of his leading Church members urged him to invite or allow me to preach, as they wished to hear me, and did not wish to be compelled to leave their own church to do it; but he absolutely refused to admit me into his pulpit on account of my abolitionism. It was not because he feared I would introduce abolitionism in my sermon, for he knew I would not do that; I never did it when I was invited to preach in a brother's pulpit. It was because he would not so far indorse the Christian character of an abolitionist as to invite him to preach in his pulpit. Being thus excluded from the Methodist pulpit, I accepted an invitation to preach in the Congregational church, and, of course, I had a large share of the Methodist congregation to hear me, and the probability is I made more abolitionists than I should if the preacher had raised no opposition, but simply pursued a let-alone policy.

I also about this time spent a week in the city of Schenectady, where I found a warm friend in the pastor of the Methodist Episcopal Church, Brother E. Goss.

My series of lectures were delivered in the Baptist Church, the pastor of which, the Rev. Mr. Sawyer, was also a warm-hearted antislavery man. Probably, considering all the circumstances, I was never more successful in delivering a series of lectures in any place than in this, and many names were added to the antislavery roll.

12

Upon my return home I spent a few days of comparative rest, delivering a few lectures in the immediate vicinity of Utica, before striking out for another extended campaign. This stay about home, however, was short, and I was soon on the wing again, as will be seen in the opening of the next chapter.

CHAPTER XIX.

Brother Brown's Trial at Auburn—My Defense—A Western Tour.

BROTHER BROWN, a member of the Church in Auburn, was put upon his trial for abolitionism. The trial commenced on the 15th of February, 1839. I was requested to act as his counsel, and contested the case to the best of my ability, for I believed him innocent of all moral wrong, and that the charges and trial were persecutions for his antislavery views and actions, which were less offensive than my own, inasmuch as he was less prominent. I have given, in a preceding chapter, a case of the trial of a minister, Rev. C. K. True, and will record this one instance as a specimen of the manner in which they tried and expelled laymen in those days. A Brother E. W. Goodwin had just been tried and expelled, to which allusion is made in this trial.

The charges were as follows:

I. Misrepresentation. Specification 1: Saying that the meeting at the organization of the Wesleyan Antislavery Society was numerously attended. Specification 2: Saying that the doctrine has recently been set up that when ministers become members of an Annual Conference they surrender the keeping of their consciences to that body, and that members yield to the Church or minister the keeping of that sacred trust.

II. Slander. Specification 1 : Representing that the Bishops of our Church would be glad to have a sword in their hands. Specification 2 : Representing that the course of our Bishops and presiding elders is anti-Methodistical. Specification 3 : Saying the pastor took away E. W. Goodwin's class-book on account of his abolitionism. Specification 4 : Saying that my course was unjust and oppressive, unwarranted by established usage and precedent, and totally at variance with the true intent and meaning of our Church Discipline. Specification 5 : Bringing my character before a public meeting, and publishing it in "Zion's Watchman."

III. Falsehood, with a design to deceive. Specification : Saying that I took away E. W. Goodwin's class-book, and deprived him of his official standing on account of his abolitionism.

Rev. W. M. Coryell, of Skaneateles, was president of the trial, by the appointment of the presiding elder. Rev. H. F. Row, pastor of the church, was complainant and prosecutor, assisted by Rev. Mr. Nash as counsel. I appeared for the accused.

I will give the points I made in summing up, with the proof offered.

It was moved by the prosecution that all the members who attended and took part in the anti-slavery prayer-meeting, which was held weekly, should be excluded from sitting on the trial, as incompetent. Of course I objected to this motion as very extraordinary, unwarrantable, and partial. My reasons were :

1. To attend and take part in an antislavery prayer-meeting could not be a disqualification to try an issue of misrepresentation, slander, and falsehood.

2. To attend an antislavery prayer-meeting could go no further than a general commitment to the principles of antislavery, which could not be a disqualification to try this case. The accused was not charged with being an antislavery man, but with misrepresentation, slander, and falsehood. To assume that all antislavery men, all who pray for the slave, cannot be trusted to try an issue of misrepresentation, slander, and falsehood, would be an outrage not to be tolerated.

3. To attend and take part in the antislavery prayer-meeting was no more a commitment in favor of the accused than staying away was a commitment against him. To be an antislavery man is not to be in favor of the accused, any more than to be opposed to antislavery is to be committed against the accused.

I honestly believed the above to be conclusive, but the chair decided otherwise, and every person who attended the antislavery prayer-meeting was stricken from the list of triers.

I then objected to the whole jury on the ground that they were the same persons who had tried the same charges in the preceding case against Brother

Goodwin. The charges were the same, the alleged acts were conjointly performed, and were sustained by the same testimony. It could not be pretended that there was any difference in the two cases. This also was overruled, and the brother was tried by those who had already decided his case against him.

I next objected to the whole proceeding as a violation of the General Rules, and read as follows:

"These are the General Rules of our Societies; if there be any among us who observe them not, who habitually breaks any of them, we will admonish him of the error of his ways. We will bear with him for a season. But if then he repent not, he hath no more place among us."

I maintained that if the charges were all well founded, they constituted the first offense, and he had never been admonished or borne with. The chair overruled my objection.

I finally objected to the trial on the ground that the brother had not been labored with, and read the rule, as follows: "In cases of neglect of duty of any kind, imprudent conduct, indulging sinful tempers and words, or disobedience to the order and discipline of the Church; first, let private reproof be given by a preacher or a leader, and if there be an acknowledgment of the fault, and proper humiliation, the person may be borne with. On a second offense the preacher or leader may take one or two faithful persons. On a third offense let the case be brought before the Society." I insisted that the charges came under this rule; that though one of them was rated higher, the specification brought it within the rule. I denied that any private labor had been bestowed on the brother, and challenged the proof, if there had been any private labor; and no proof was offered, and yet the chair overruled my objection.

The proof offered is all given in the following statement of my summing up of the case:

First charge, "Misrepresentation."

First specification: "Saying that the meeting at the organization of the Wesleyan Antislavery Society was numerously attended."

The statement is admitted, and its truth is affirmed. "Numerously" is a relative term, and, at best, is a matter of opinion. It has been proved by a witness, who was not present, but who was sent to measure the room preparatory to testifying in this trial, that the room where the meeting was held was eighteen feet by thirty. It has been proved by a witness, who was present at the meeting, and was led to count, on account of there being so many more than usual, that there were fifty persons. It was then, I affirm, in its relations to such meetings generally, a numerously attended meeting.

Second specification: "Saying that the doctrine has recently been set up, that when ministers become members of an Annual Conference they surrender the keeping of their consciences to that body," etc.

The statement was admitted, and I offered to prove it true, but was not allowed so to do. The chair simply said it would not admit of proof, and that no attempt to prove it could be allowed. Of course, I could only affirm in my summing up what I would have proved if allowed. I affirmed that the doctrine alleged was set up in the New York Conference, in the trial of the Rev. C. K. True, and the Rev. John Kennaday affirmed, during that trial, that when he joined that Conference, he committed the keeping of his conscience to the Conference.

I urged, that if it was untrue, no person was misrepresented, for no person or body of persons was named as having set up the doctrine, and no time and place were named when and where it was done.

I also urged that many other persons believed just what the brother had affirmed, insomuch that at most it is a matter of opinion, held by many others in common with himself, for which he cannot be condemned for misrepresentation.

Second charge, " Slander."

First specification: " Representing that the Bishops of our Church would be glad to have a sword in their hands."

This charge was denied, and all the proof adduced was that the defendant said that he was glad that the Bishops had not a sword. I contended in my argument that the evidence did not sustain the specification, and that the specification did not sus-

tain the charge of slander. It would not be slander
if true.

Second specification : " Representing that the course
of our Bishops and presiding elders is anti-Methodistical."

In my defense I argued,

1. What Methodism is, and what constitutes anti-
Methodism, are matters of opinion among Methodists
themselves, and members, ministers, and administrators disagree. It cannot, therefore, be slander.

2. No particular act or acts were named as being
anti-Methodistical, and it was, therefore, no slander,
unless it be slander to call in question the infallibility
of the administration of our Bishops and presiding
elders.

3. No one Bishop or presiding elder was referred
to, so no one could be slandered.

Third specification : " Saying that the pastor took
away E. W. Goodwin's class-book on account of his
abolitionism."

Two competent and creditable witnesses testified
that the plaintiff told them that he took away Goodwin's class-book on account of his abolitionism. I
also offered the affidavit of Goodwin himself, but the
chair would not receive it.

In summing up I argued that, as it was positively
proved that the class-book was taken away on account
of the abolitionism of the holder, it could be no slander to report it, unless the slander grew out of the

fact that it was damaging to the plaintiff's character to have it known that he took away a class-book for such a cause; and if this be allowed, if you convict the defendant, you will tenfold more condemn your minister by saying that he has done what it is a slander even to report.

Fourth specification: "Saying that my course was unjust and oppressive, unwarranted by established usage and precedent, and totally at variance with the true intent and meaning of our Church Discipline."

On this specification, I remarked that there was not the slightest doubt that the defendant honestly believed that the preacher's conduct was all that he had affirmed it to be, and many others believed the same— that I did myself; and to arraign a member on such a matter of opinion, where so many agreed with him, was adding to his acts of oppression. As to established usage and precedent, there could be none, for the occasion and course were new; it had been reserved for the opposers of abolitionism to perform such acts.

Fifth specification: "Bringing my character before a public meeting, and publishing it in 'Zion's Watchman.'"

I insisted that the defendant never brought the character of the plaintiff before a public meeting; that the charge was based upon a resolution adopted by a meeting at which defendant presided, and he neither introduced it, discussed it, nor voted for it. The meeting voted that the proceedings be published, signed by the chairman and secretary, and he put his name to the document, and had only signed the paper in compliance with the vote of the meeting. I further urged, that the whole matter charged was not a slander. It is not necessarily a slander to bring a man's character before a public meeting, and to publish him in "Zion's Watchman." Slander or no slander, he was in a fair way to get published again, for such proceedings as the present need a public ventilation.

Third charge, "Falsehood, with a design to deceive."

Specification: "Saying that I took away E. W. Goodwin's class-book, and deprived him of his official standing on account of his abolitionism."

I remarked that the fact alleged in this count is the same that is charged as slander in the third specification, under the charge of slander. It is saying that the class-book was taken from Goodwin for his abolitionism. The evidence and the arguments on that specification are equally applicable here, and need not be repeated. The additional charge of an intention to deceive is fallacious. There is not the slightest doubt that the defendant and many others believed the statement, and believing it, a design to deceive any one could not have constituted the motive for reporting it. Brother Brown had stood high as a Christian, and had always been true to the Church; and, in closing my defense, I made an appeal, under which some of the triers wept aloud, but it did not save him; there was enough of the non-weeping sort to do the work assigned them, and they convicted him; though my defense, or something else, made a decided improvement on this trial over that of Goodwin, which had preceded it.

The following was the verdict:

First charge, "Misrepresentation." First specification, "Not guilty." Second specification, "Guilty."

Second charge, "Slander." First specification, "Not guilty." Second specification, "Guilty of slander in the second degree, which acquits Brother Brown of all intentional wrong." Third specification, "Not guilty." Fourth specification, "Guilty of slander in the second degree, which acquits Brother Brown of all intentional wrong." Fifth specification, "Not guilty."

Third charge, "Falsehood, with a design to deceive." Specification, "Saying that I took away E. W. Goodwin's class-book, and deprived him of his official standing on account of his abolitionism." "Not guilty."

From this rendering it is seen that the accused was acquitted of all guilt except on one count out of eight, namely, guilty of misrepresentation in saying that the doctrine had been set up that preachers committed the keeping of their consciences to the Conference. Upon this finding the chairman rose and pronounced the defendant expelled from the Church.

These things made an impression on my mind. I saw clearly that there was really no security for the standing of abolitionists in the Church. The two cases in which I had acted as counsel were not the only like cases which were occurring in various places, and I began to ask myself, "What will the end of these things be?" I began to reflect what could be done if a time should come when a different course of action from that which I was pursuing should be demanded. It looked as though abolitionists would ultimately be crushed out of the Church. Some would submit, but others would not, and I should be found with the non-submitting class, and what then? I did not dare to attempt an answer.

There was one circumstance which occurred during the trial that was a small satisfaction to me, and perhaps to some others. I was well known in Auburn; I had preached in their pulpit during the session of Conference, and there was a strong desire to hear me. The trial was so protracted that it was clear I would remain over the Sabbath, and the brethren urged their pastor to consent to let me occupy the pulpit; but he absolutely refused. The Rev. Mr. Hopkins, of the First Presbyterian Church, sent word to me that if I would preach for him on Sunday morning, I might occupy his pulpit in the evening for an antislavery lecture. I accepted, and the result was there were very few people at the Methodist church either morning or evening.

From Auburn I went westward on a lecturing tour. I lectured in the Congregational church in Canandaigua, one of the most aristocratic places in western New York. There were some symptoms of trouble, and some of the timid ones became alarmed. The house was full, though it was on a week-day afternoon. When expectation of trouble was at its highest, just as the last of the throng were crowding in, I rose and commenced reading a hymn from the Methodist Hymn Book:

"Shall I, for fear of feeble man,
The Spirit's course in me restrain?"

and I read it with such a pathos that I believe it awed opposers, and I know it scattered the fears of the timid. We had no disturbance. I went as far as Warsaw, Wyoming County. My principal object was to attend a county antislavery convention, which was to be held there. The anniversary of the County Bible Society occurred during the same week, and the Methodist quarterly meeting also was held on the following Saturday and Sunday. Altogether it made an interesting week. I was invited to make a speech in the Bible meeting, which I did. I stayed over the Sabbath, but could have no part in the quarterly meeting. The presiding elder, the Rev. Mr. Alverson, was one of the peculiar abolition haters who would not have any thing to do with abolitionists. The brethren urged him to let me occupy the pulpit on Sunday evening, but he absolutely refused, saying that he should preach himself. This, every body knew, was to keep me out of the pulpit, for he was not in the habit of preaching but one sermon on Sunday. He consented that I might use the pulpit at two o'clock P. M. The brethren accepted on my behalf, not knowing the elder's offer was a plan to defeat me. At the morning service he sung long meter, prayed long meter, administered the sacrament long meter, and by the time he had got through with all these long meters it was two o'clock, and he supposed the people were tired and must go home, and that I could get no hearing. Such conduct was not to go unpunished. A goodly number stayed, perhaps some of them out of spite. Others came in, and I had quite a respectable though small congregation. I preached as well as I could, and at the close of my sermon I told them I would preach in the Congregational church in the evening. The result was the presiding elder, Alverson, had only nine to hear him preach, and one of them was one of my friends who went there to count them.

I then returned home, having lectured on my way out in a number of places not named, and I also delivered several lectures by the way on my return. Spring was now opening, and I spent several weeks in the vicinity of home, visiting and lecturing in places within ten and fifteen miles of Utica.

CHAPTER XX.

Home Work—Egg Logic—A Tour East—A Tour North—
Home again—Having Closed my Year's Labor, I Resign
my Agency.

AFTER my return from the western part of the
State I spent a few weeks lecturing in the vicinity of home. Only one of these efforts is entitled
to special notice.

I sent forward an appointment to lecture in the
town of Floyd on a week-day evening. As it was
entirely a rural neighborhood there was no thought
of any disturbance. There was a wealthy farmer living
near the church who was called Col. Pomeroy, said
to be a leading Methodist. As I was an entire
stranger, I called upon him and announced myself as
the lecturer. He was far from being an abolitionist,
yet he was a gentleman, and received me kindly, and
said his house should be my welcome home while I
remained. He had known me by reputation through
the press and otherwise, and was willing to hear me
on the great question, though he differed from me.

The church was a large, old-fashioned one, with a
very high pulpit with a door on each side, and a large
window at the preacher's back, as he stood in the pulpit and faced the audience. This exposed the preach-

er to the view of those who might stand in front of the house in the evening when the pulpit was lighted. In the midst of my lecture there came a volley of eggs through the window on my back, hurled by a company of disturbers who had gathered in front of the house. They were sent with such violence through the glass as to sound like the discharge of pistols or guns. For the moment I did not understand what the racket was, but I soon learned. The pulpit was so high as to compel them to elevate their ordnance so high, in order to shoot through the window, that all passed over my head, and took effect about midway in the congregation, and some ladies and gentlemen received all the eggs which were intended for me. The eggs were not addled, as were the brains of those who sent them. It was too early in the spring for bad eggs. The moment the racket began, my host, Col. Pomeroy, sprang for the door, and being a very powerful man, and very much excited, I would not have gone security for the rascals had his way been clear; but they had taken the precaution to tie both doors on the outside, and they made their escape before he could get out. The congregation coming to order, I remarked that the miscreants, by fastening the doors, had saved their bacon, and had better have saved their eggs, and then finished my lecture.

The spring having now opened, and the ground being settled, I started on another lecturing tour, and passed through Herkimer County into Schoharie

County, lecturing at all feasible places. In Schoharie, where I was born, I found but one person who knew any thing of me, and that was a friend who had moved from Delaware County, where I had been brought up. I left there when a child, and some of the facts of moving were among the first abiding records my memory had made. All foot-prints made, not only by my own little feet, but by the whole family, had been blotted out by thirty-nine years; yet there stood some of the old stone buildings which were there when the place, in its infancy, was assaulted and sacked by Tories and Indians during the war of the Revolution.

From Schoharie I shaped my course for Albany, lecturing by the way. I made a principal effort at Rensselaerville, where I spent a Sabbath and preached in the Methodist Episcopal church, and gave several lectures. While stopping here I found a home with Brother Raymond, the father of Rev. Dr. Miner Raymond. I received the following anecdote from his own lips: Mr. Raymond was a farmer, whose farm was on the hill high above and a mile or two from the stream that ran through the valley below, whither he had to drive his sheep for washing every spring. In the early discussion of the temperance question Mr. Raymond was inclined to be a temperance man, but did not see how he could sign the pledge and keep it, as he really believed it impossible to go into cold water and wash sheep without whisky and not be sick. The time of sheep-washing came, and he secured his help, and got his large flock of sheep down into the valley, and in the yard upon the bank of the stream, and preparatory to beginning a drink must be taken by all hands. He lifted his quart bottle full of the good creature to take the first drink, when it slipped from his hand and fell upon a stone and was broken, and every drop was lost. What could be done? He could not well take his flock back upon the hill and bring them down another day, and no liquor could be obtained without sending miles for it. On a moment's reflection he resolved to run the risk of washing sheep without liquor, if he could persuade his help to take the hazard with him. He said to his men: " You see, boys, how it is; I will add twenty-five cents apiece to your wages to make up for the spilt whisky, and let us wash the sheep and have done with it." All consented, and the work was accomplished, and instead of being sick the next day, he had never before felt so well after sheep-washing, and he concluded the use of liquor injured men more in the water than it did out of it, and he signed the pledge and never again used or furnished liquor on any occasion.

When I reached Albany I crossed the Hudson River and lectured in Greenbush, and from thence went north into Washington County, and lectured in all the principal places in the county, and wound up with a county antislavery meeting at Union Village.

Here I met Gerrit Smith, who came to attend the convention. As there were some present who knew no better than to oppose abolition and to defend slavery, there was some music and a little fun.

After the convention I crossed the Hudson River and lectured several evenings in a Baptist church in the neighborhood of the Stillwater battle-field, of Revolutionary fame, and at some other places in the vicinity, after which I started for home, passing through Saratoga and Johnstown.

Summer was now at its full strength, and after spending a short time at home, during which I delivered several lectures in the villages and neighborhoods within reaching distance of Utica, I started on another tour to the north and north-east, in company with Mr. Chaplin, the general agent of the State society. We passed through Lewis, Jefferson, and St. Lawrence Counties, into Franklin County, and then returned through the same counties, mainly by another route. We usually divided the time, each speaking to the several congregations that came out to hear us. Nothing occurred during this campaign worthy of special note, more than that we passed over the territory of several of my pastoral charges and theological battle-fields of other days. Some of my former friends did not know me, and others scowled, so great was the difference between a Methodist preacher in his regular work, defending Methodism, and the same Methodist preacher when defending the rights of humanity, and pleading for the dumb and downtrodden. I am happy to say this remark does not apply to all. I met with many warm greetings, and enjoyed much pleasure in meeting with my old friends.

When I again reached home autumn had come, with his sear leaf and chilling winds, and, having performed my year's labor for the Society, I resigned my agency, much to the regret of the Executive Committee, as they took occasion to express themselves.

CHAPTER XXI.

A Brief Review—A Specimen of my Principles and Mode of Presenting them.

I HAVE now devoted a year to the antislavery cause, and those who have read the record of the same will not pronounce it a year of idleness and ease, and I know it has not been a money-making labor. I know that my motive has been to save my country from the disgrace and guilt of slavery, and the Church from its pollution and rottenness. I started out with a love for the Church which impelled me to seek her purity by the removal of slavery from her communion. And yet my motives have been impugned, I have been slandered, shunned, and apparently hated by those who had been my best friends, and I have been assailed by mob violence. Why has it been so? I have not intended to give any unnecessary offense. In discussing so great an evil, I have undoubtedly used strong language, but no stronger than true. That the generation that shall come after me may judge between me and those from whom I have received such treatment, I will here record one of the most severe speeches I ever made. It was delivered in the Broadway Tabernacle, in New York, at the anniversary of the American

Antislavery Society, May, 1832, in response to the following resolution, which I was requested to present:

Resolved, That American slavery usurps the prerogatives of God, tends to blot the divine image from the soul of man, degrades him below the rank his Maker assigned him in the scale of creation, and subverts all the social relations which God and nature have made essential.

Mr. President: Were I to attempt to give a brief but comprehensive view of the sinfulness of slavery I would do it in the words of St. Paul to Bar-jesus: "O full of all subtilty and all mischief, thou child of the devil, thou enemy of all righteousness, wilt thou not cease to pervert the right ways of the Lord?" And then I would answer the question in an emphatic NO, that would make every heart feel that slavery is so bad that it is beyond being made better. I do not so undervalue the intelligence and moral sense and humanity of this assembly as to suppose that they are pro-slavery in judgment, heart, and feeling; yet as there is a vast difference between believing that slavery is wrong and seeing and feeling how great a wrong it is, I trust it will give no offense to take it for granted that there are many in this vast assembly who have not fully considered the magnitude of this great sin. I wish to be understood as not making this effort so much to convince your judgments that slavery is wrong as to cause you to see and feel the greatness of the wrong, that its guilt rises as high as heaven and that its corruption is as deep as hell.

The resolution which I have the honor of presenting charges slavery with four distinct crimes, which I will attempt to sustain:

I. Slavery is charged with usurping the prerogatives of God. To sustain this I need only compare the claims of God with the claims of slave-holders. The claim of God is stated in these words: "Thou shalt love the Lord thy God with all thy heart, and with all thy soul, and with all thy mind, and with all thy strength." The claim of the slave-holder is stated in the following words of the Civil Code of Louisiana: "A slave is one who is in the power of a master to whom he belongs. The master may sell him, dispose of his person, his industry and labor: he can do nothing, and possess nothing, nor acquire any thing but what must belong to his master." The slave-holder clearly claims what God has reserved for himself, and usurps God's prerogatives. The slave-holder seizes upon the subjects of God's moral government and wrests them from their allegiance to his throne, and takes them out of his administrative hand, and subjects them to the absolute will of a despot who is not satisfied with trampling upon the rights of man, but attempts to wrest the reins of government from the hand of Him whose throne is in the heavens. The claim of the slave-holder equals the claim of God; it claims the whole man, and asserts an absolute right to body and soul, muscle and mind, all that the man is, all that he can do, all that he can possess, and all that he can acquire. God can claim no more, and it is plain that the slave-holder's claim takes all and leaves nothing to satisfy God's claim. Suppose a slave obeys God so far as he can in his circumstances, and believes in Christ, and secures eternal life, will that belong to his owner? He claims all his slave can do and acquire. Will he appear when crowns are distributed and claim it? Or suppose the slave is as wicked as his master and dies an heir of hell, will the master be entitled to his slave's wages of sin? "He can do nothing, and possess nothing, nor acquire any thing but what must belong to his master."

It is seen that slavery robs men of the power and means of obeying God. Can a slave who is in the power of a master, and who can do nothing but what must belong to his master, obey God on his own account? It is impossible. Can a slave who "can possess nothing, nor acquire any thing but what must belong to his master," visit the sick, feed the hungry, and clothe the naked? You all know he cannot, and hence you know that slavery disqualifies a man to be a subject of God's moral government; it denies the means of obeying the most simple precepts of the Gospel; it therefore contravenes the claims of God, and sets at naught the great law of our being which holds all intelligent beings in allegiance to their Creator. If this is not treason against the government of God treason cannot exist. If it is not trespass upon the prerogatives of God it cannot be proved that the devil has committed trespass in the case of all the souls he has seduced from their allegiance to the divine throne; for he never claimed more than slavery claims, and never received more from the most zealous fiend that ever served his cause, disembodied or incarnate—no, not in hell, where he rules perverted immortality under the cloud of darkness that mantles the damned. How damning, then, must be the guilt of slavery! It is the sum of all sin, a monopoly of crime. For a man to attempt to throw off his own allegiance to his Maker is a crime fearful to contemplate; but how much more fearful is the crime of slavery, which lays hold of millions, and steps in between them and the government of God! The common sin of refusing to obey God is swallowed up and lost sight of in the slave-holder's greater crime, who not only refuses to obey, but refuses to allow others to obey, seizing upon the subjects of God's government and appropriating them to his own use, body and mind, intellect, will, and conscience, without leaving one reserved power or right to the claim of God. It is, then, clear that slavery usurps the prerogatives of God, and so far as it succeeds in enforcing its principles the government of God is blotted from the world.

II. The resolution charges slavery with a tendency to blot the divine image from the soul of man. Without discussing metaphysically the question as to what constitutes the image of God in man, I will say that it includes all mental and moral endowments which distinguish men from brutes and ally them to and make them like God.

1. While brutes were created with inferior spirits that go downward, man claims affinity with the world above, God having added to his earthly nature a living soul, which was infused of his own immortal breath. It is admitted that slavery can never render man less than immortal by blotting out this likeness of God's immortality, yet it overlooks it and treats him as though he was not immortal, and as having no higher destiny than brutes that perish, no future more than the horse or the ox. This image of God, this living soul which God kindled in man with the quenchless fires of his own immortality, is made a personal chattel to be bought and sold in the market, to be used for the exclusive benefit of the purchaser, as an instrument to gratify his love of gold, power, or lust, as his propensities may dictate. Slavery degrades this immortal man to a level with the ox and mule, to toil with them under the sting of the driver's lash from life's cloudy dawn to its dark going down, as though the negro has no heaven to hope for beyond his dream, too soon disturbed by the sound of the driver's horn summoning him to a renewal of his unrequited toil; and no hell to fear beyond the tortures of the cotton-field, the sugar plantation, or the rice swamp.

2. While God created brutes with an instinctive

nature to guide them, he endowed man with the higher faculty of reason, and thus modeled him after his own image, he alone possessing reason absolutely perfect and eternal. This noble power of reason slavery blots out, or suppresses only so much as can make them useful as beasts of burden or instruments of menial toil. Slave-holders know that human beings cannot be held in slavery without also being held in ignorance; hence laws are enacted which make it a penal offense to teach a slave to read, and every possible effort is made to keep them in darkest ignorance. They must live and die in ignorance of God's holy word. They may not be taught to read the revelation which God has given for a light to the life of all men. It is made a crime to give a Bible to a slave. Let your Bible Society send out its agent to distribute the word of God, and let him attempt to approach the slave quarters with a Bible in his hand, and slavery will lift up its snaky head and lap out its forked tongue and tell him he must not go there. Thus slavery does all it can to blot the image of God from the souls of men. Spirits which God created capable of endless improvement, and destined to fill and illume a celestial sphere, slavery consigns to a night of ignorance as enduring as life and as rayless as the brow of despair.

III. The resolution charges slavery with degrading man from the dignified rank assigned him in the scale of creation. God placed man over the work of his hands, saying, "Let them have dominion over the fish of the sea, and over the fowl of the air, and over the cattle, and over all the earth." This glory and honor with which God crowned his creature man, slavery plucks from his brow; it robs him of the authority with which the Creator invested him, and with its profane and heaven-daring hand hurls him down from the sphere assigned him by the Almighty, and gives him a place among the brutes that perish.

All the rights and authority which God gave to the first man belong equally to all men, because they were bestowed upon the common father of all the race. God "hath made of one blood all nations of men for to dwell on all the face of the earth," and it was when the blood of all men—white, red, and black —flowed undistinguished in the veins of a common father, and rushed through its arterial course at the pulsations of the one individual heart, that God crowned man with the right to possess and rule the world; and hence the right of possession and control belongs to all men, without distinction of color or nationality. This right is wrested from the slave, for the law of slavery will not allow him to possess or rule any thing, not even himself, not even his own hands and feet. God says to the colored man no less than to the white man, "Have dominion over the fish of the sea, and over the fowl of the air, and over the cattle, and over all the earth;" but slavery says,

" Not so, Lord; the slave can do nothing, and possess nothing, nor acquire any thing but what must belong to his master." Now, which tells the truth, God or the slave code ?

IV. The resolution charges slavery with subverting the social relations of man, which, in the constitution of nature, God has rendered essential to his existence. Man is a social being; the Creator formed him for social life by giving him a nature which claims and receives social enjoyments from kindred spirits. God having created man to live in social relations, has given us rules for the government of these relations; and the charge is that slavery annuls these rules and subverts these relations, and pours a full cup of wormwood and gall into the very fountains of human society.

1. Slavery strikes down the divine law of marriage, annuls the relation of husband and wife, and renders the entire intercourse among slaves an unmitigated system of fornication, adultery, or concubinage. Marriage, as instituted by God, is the fountain of social life, which sends out its living streams of social animation to bless and make joyful what would otherwise be a desert and cheerless world. This institution is the first and oldest known to humanity; its plan was laid when God said, " It is not good that man should be alone ;" it was carried into practical actuality when God, having formed a woman, presented her to the man, fair and innocent, amid the

floral charms of Eden's undefiled bowers, before depravity had corrupted the fountain of the heart, or one blush of guilt and shame had flushed the face of humanity. It is upon this first union of one man with one woman that Christ says, "For this cause shall a man leave father and mother, and shall cleave to his wife: and they twain shall be one flesh. . . . What therefore God hath joined together, let not man put asunder." In violation of this, slavery lays its sacrilegious hand upon the bridal pair and rends them asunder as though God had not joined them together. But it may admit of a question whether they are joined together or not. No matter; if they are joined together by God, then slavery actually severs bonds that are divine. If they are not joined together by God they are not married in a scriptural sense, and slavery stands convicted of breaking up the marriage institution altogether, and the three millions of slaves present one field of corruption, pollution, and rottenness. The advocates of slavery may take which horn of the dilemma they please. If they are married, slavery puts asunder those whom God hath joined together; if slaves are not married, slavery is guilty of subverting entirely a divinely appointed institution.

What a mockery is any pretended marriage of slaves! Let the slave give the only true answer the case will admit of, and the ceremony will be something as follows:

Question. "Wilt thou have this woman to be thy wedded wife?"

Answer. "Master says I may, or must, as the case may be."

Quest. "Wilt thou love her and keep her?"

Ans. "Master keeps her for me; I cannot keep myself; master keeps us both."

Quest. "Wilt thou keep thee only unto her so long as ye both shall live?"

Ans. "I will if master does not separate us by selling us apart."

Quest. "Wilt thou have this man to be thy wedded husband? Wilt thou keep thee only unto him so long as ye both shall live?"

Ans. "I will if master, some of his boys, his overseer, or some other white man does not step in between us and force me to break my promise, as I have no right to resist or lift my hand against any white man."

2. Slavery annuls the obligations growing out of the relation of parents and children. The command of God is, "Children, obey your parents in the Lord;" but slavery says, "Not so, Lord; they must obey their masters, who own them, who may separate them at pleasure by selling the parents upon the auction-block, and children by the pound." The son may not obey his father, out of whose loins he came; he may not obey him in childhood; may not support him in manhood; may not wipe a tear from his pa-

rent's sorrowful eye, or reach out his hand to steady his tottering gait as he totters down life's declivity, hastened by the sting of the slave-driver's lash. The daughter may not obey her mother, who in anguish gave her being; may not pour one drop of consolation into the grief-charged bosom, from which she drew her first nutriment, and at which she was nurtured in helpless infancy, and reared to endure the woes of womanhood's years.

God commands parents to train up their children "in the nurture and admonition of the Lord," but slavery says, "Not so, Lord; they must train up their children, or leave them to grow up for me, that I may sacrifice their sons upon the altar of my avarice, and their daughters upon the altar of my lust."

I believe I have fully sustained the resolution, yet I do not pretend that I have fully revealed all the horrors of slavery in its bloody work and damning guilt. I have only discovered to you the tips of the serpent's forked tongue; the body of the viper, in awful magnitude and hideous form, lies concealed, and is known only in the ever-present miseries, the unfathomable anguish and untellable horrors of the cotton-field, the sugar plantation, and the rice swamp, from which I will not attempt to lift the veil. Let no one suppose I have exaggerated the sin of slavery; exaggeration is impossible; the simple truth transcends the power of fiction, and every attempt at declamation must lessen and lighten the cloud of

14

dark terrors that ever hang over and shroud the slave system. To describe slavery would require a language which would combine words expressive of the shrieking terrors of death, the gloom of rayless despair, and the glowing fires of hell. Could I call up the winds of the South and cause them to pour into the ears of this assembly the sighs and shrieks and groans of tortured fathers and tortured mothers and tortured sons and tortured daughters, I should need no other argument, for these outbursts of suffering and terror concentrating in your ears would sound as loud and wild as the cry of assembled ghosts. But I will forbear, or in my conception of the great evil of slavery I shall substitute execration for argument. As Michael, when contending with the devil, brought not a railing accusation against him, but said, "The Lord rebuke thee," so I say, May the Lord rebuke slavery, and rebuke it as Christ rebuked intruding devils, which sent them back in scampering haste to their own hell; and may it not, like the ejected legion, be permitted to enter into the swine, but be driven, naked and unattended, down the gulf of everlasting chaos and oblivion, never more to lift its serpentine head this side of the bourn which divides this from the world of the unblessed. Let it be blotted from the polluted records of the Church; let it be blotted from the disgraced annals of the State and Nation; and if it must have an enduring page assigned it upon which to record its existence and doings, let it be in the biography of some chief among damned spirits, or in the history of Beelzebub, the prince of the devils.

The above has been given as a specimen of my mode of attacking slavery, and I may affirm, with all truth and sincerity, that in no lecture was I more severe or provoking than in the above address. It was not, however, my severity or mode of treating the subject which caused me to be mobbed, for those who mobbed me never heard me.

CHAPTER XXII.

Invited to Massachusetts—Made a Lecturing Tour through
Connecticut—Middletown—Reached Boston very Sick.

I WAS invited by the Massachusetts Society to become their General Agent, and answered favorably and told them I would visit Boston in a few weeks and close a contract if we could agree. I had also been urged to visit Connecticut, and concluded to make a lecturing tour through that State on my way to Boston. I started in September, 1839, and lectured in Meriden and various other places until I reached Middletown, the seat of the Wesleyan University, where I had been strongly urged to come. There was a strong antislavery feeling in the city, and there were several young men among the students that were very decided in their antislavery views. Among these was the young man who has grown to be Rev. Dr. R. S. Rust, the present General Agent of the Freedmen's Aid Society. It was proposed that I should deliver a series of lectures in the Congregational church, as the Methodist church was not open for antislavery lectures. There was no bell in the Congregational church, and the Methodist bell, by way of courtesy, was usually rung for meetings in the Congregational church. The bell was rung for my first lecture, as it had been for other meetings. This so roused the spirit of the pastor, the Rev. Francis Hodgson, that he rushed into the church and stopped the ringing, and forbade the sexton to ring the bell any more for my lectures. This so exasperated the friends of free discussion that a subscription was circulated, and a sufficient amount was secured to purchase a bell for the Congregational church. In my lectures I defended myself against the charge of being a disturber and a slanderer of the Church by attacking and exposing the pro-slavery position of the Church. This so excited the Rev. Mr. Hodgson that he sent me a challenge to meet him in a public debate.

This just suited me, for I knew I had the right side of the subject, and that I understood it, and could make capital for the cause out of a public debate. I accepted, and the news spread, and when the evening came for the debate to open the house was crowded. I went in and took my seat, but Mr. Hodgson did not appear. After waiting a few moments one of the professors from the university rose and stated that he appeared in the place of Mr. Hodgson, authorized to withdraw his challenge. He stated, further, that it was not Mr. Hodgson's wish to decline the debate ; that they had with difficulty persuaded him to consent to have it withdrawn. Mr. Hodgson was very ardent and anxious for the debate, but they were aware that he would meet Mr. Lee at great disadvantage, as he had made the subject a specialty for a long time and understood it in all its bearings, whereas Mr. Hodgson had paid but little attention to it, and could not meet Mr. Lee on equal ground. I rose and bowed as gracefully as I knew how to the professor, and stated that I accepted of his apology for Mr. Hodgson; that he had a right to challenge me; had a right to withdraw his challenge; and, as I had spent no time and labor in making special preparation for the debate, I had no reason to complain. But, as the challenge was now withdrawn, I was at liberty to resume my lectures, and would avail myself of the occasion to deliver the next in the series. Without any further allusion to the challenge, I proceeded with my lecture as though nothing unusual had occurred.

Having closed my lectures in Middletown, I started for Boston. I became very sick on the way, with unquestionable symptoms of a settled fever. I had felt unwell for a day or two; now I perfectly understood my case. I had a fever. I had the names of a few friends in Boston, but there was no person in the city I had ever seen. I reached Boston late in the night and went to a hotel, and waited until morning, when, being too sick to leave my room, I dispatched messages to some of my friends, for though I had no acquaintances, there were friends, if I could get word to them. The first man who responded to my messages was the Rev. Dexter King. He notified others, who came to see me, and on consultation I was removed from the hotel to the infirmary of

ex-Rev. Elias Smith, the father of the noted Matthew
Hale Smith.   Here I was treated for several days, but,
becoming dissatisfied with the mode of treatment,
Mr. Bracket, of Charlestown, came with his carriage
and removed me to his own house.   I had become
so feeble it was with difficulty I could be moved ;
but the thing was accomplished, a physician was
called, and I had the best of care.   The fever was
still running its course, but after a few days it began
to abate, and grew less and less until it left me entirely.   My physician said my remarkable constitution
was too much for the fever, and wore it out and con-
quered it without allowing it to come to a crisis.   I
felt that there had been a severe battle, and that I
had been rather roughly handled.   I recovered very
rapidly after the fever left, or, as the physician said,
was worn out.   While yet quite feeble I started for
home and arrived safely, and was soon as vigorous
as ever, and ready to renew the battle.   I was soon
on my way to Boston with my family, and settled
them in Charlestown, near Boston, and was ready to
take the field.   It was now late in November, 1839,
and I went to work with a will.

CHAPTER XXIII.

My New Field of Labor—Difficulties in the way of Rapid Progress—A Triangular Fight.

THERE were now two antislavery societies in Massachusetts. A portion of the antislavery men were now turning their attention to political action against slavery, which was vehemently opposed by another portion, and among them some of the strongest and most popular. William Lloyd Garrison and Wendell Phillips and others condemned all political action, and declared it a sin to vote under the proslavery Constitution of the United States. This, and some other causes, produced a division, and a new society was organized in Massachusetts, composed mainly of those who believed in political action against slavery; and it was this new society that I had engaged to serve, and it placed me in the front rank of the battle.

Relatively to politics there were three parties in the field : the old society, led by Mr. Garrison and others; the new society, which I served as General Agent; and the two political parties, Whigs and Democrats, who opposed the political antislavery party as bitterly as they did each other. We were approaching the presidential campaign of 1840, of which something more will be said hereafter. Placed between the two great political parties on one side, and the non-voting, non-resistant antislavery party on the other, we had warm work.

But there was another element that entered into the triangular and confused battle; a large portion of the old antislavery society had also become antichurch. Many of their most prominent speakers and writers not only opposed the pro-slavery position of the Churches, but denounced all Church organizations as wrong, wicked, and the greatest enemies of God and humanity. My own position on all these questions stood out well-defined. In New York I had strongly committed myself to political action against slavery. In the convention held in Albany, in May, 1839, I made an argument for political action which some said turned the scale in favor of a political antislavery party, and with this prestige I came to Massachusetts. I was never utopian enough to give any quarter to non-resistance, or to suppose that humanity can exist in social relations without civil government; or that we can secure a right government without right voting. On the Church question my views were fully known. I believed in the necessity and Christian duty of maintaining Church organizations, and Church relations, fellowship, and communion. While I denounced the pro-slavery position and action of some of the Churches, I never failed to throw my whole strength and influence in favor of

Church organizations, and defended them on all proper occasions.

These unequivocal positions, while they gave self-reliance and helped my courage, and rendered what friends I had decisive, made me a target for the shafts of pro-slavery politicians, and all non-political, non-voting, non-resistance, non-Church antislavery men. Thus I went into the battle in Massachusetts in the autumn of 1839.

The first contest was for the control of the local societies. When there came to be two State societies, the county, city, and town societies had to decide with which they would act; and, as they were often found divided, severe contests arose out of the question, and each State society did what it could to assist its friends in these local contests. This strife was in progress when I entered upon my agency. As this, and some other questions which often intruded, did not belong to the great issue between slavery and liberty, I will say what seems necessary at this point, and dismiss them before I attempt to present an outline of my year's labor.

The first contest in which I took a part was at the annual meeting of the Barnstable County Society, at which time it was understood they would decide with which State society they would act. Both parties rallied. The old society was represented by Mr. Collins, the General Agent. I appeared for the new society, assisted by the Rev. C. T. Torrey, a

Congregational minister. Mr. Torrey being an able debater, and well known, and I being an entire stranger, I induced him to open the debate, and drew their fire. That this was the best policy was evidenced in the summing up of the matter. I made no set speech, but only threw an occasional bomb to stir up their batteries, until their arguments appeared exhausted, when I took the floor and made the best argument I was capable of making. Mr. Collins saw that if the vote was taken his cause would be lost, and he sprang upon the floor and made an effort to get the question put over for another meeting of the society, insisting that the question had been much complicated, and that they had not paid sufficient attention to the subject, were not prepared for a final vote, and that by putting the question over they could inform themselves and reach a more deliberate and satisfactory conclusion. Barnstable County is down on Cape Cod, and while there may be no locality in Massachusetts where the sun does not shine, it is as much obscured by the mists of the cape as in any part of the State. I replied in a few words by inquiring if Mr. Collins designed to insult that intelligent congregation by telling them that they did not understand the subject, did not know what they wanted, that they had come together to do a work they did not understand, and must go home and study and learn what they wanted to do, and come again. I trusted they would show at once by their votes that they understood what they wanted better than he could tell them. The vote was taken, and, of course, I won by a large majority.

These contests over local organizations did not leave the ladies undisturbed. The Ladies' Antislavery Society of Boston maintained a severe struggle for a long time, each party rallying in all their strength at each meeting, until a decisive vote was finally obtained. In this fight I had no personal part, yet my better half was drawn into it, and did her part, at least in voting, when the battle ended in the triumph of the new society party, showing that a majority of the ladies were in favor of civil government, of voting, of resistance, when it is necessary, and of Church organization. The non-resistant, no-Church, and come-out elements often gathered in conventions of their own in those days. These were absolutely open to free discussion, and all who were disposed to do so had a perfect right to go in and take part in the discussions. Myself and two particular friends, a Baptist and a Congregationalist minister, often constituted a trio in those conventions, on account of the opportunity it gave us to expose non-resistance, and to defend the Church, the ministry, the Sabbath, and even Christianity itself. In one of them I tried my steel on the sword of Theodore Parker, in defense of the inspiration of the Scriptures. In another one of my friends defended the Christian ministry from an assault, by showing that there were ten outspoken antislavery ministers to one layman, in proportion to the whole number of both classes. It silenced the whole convention for that time.

In another of those conventions we, the trio, drew our swords, each in turn, and flashed them in the face of the convention, in defense of the Christian Sabbath. Those efforts were not lost.

Often the wildest views would come to the surface, and would provoke a reply that furnished amusement for those who could enjoy a sharp retort. I indulged in this myself on one occasion. The first battle was over the organization of the convention. A strong party was opposed to all organization, and resisted the election of a chairman. During this contest my friends and I took advantage of the state of things to make the attempt to do business without organization appear ridiculous. Finally the convention was organized by the election of Josiah Quincy as chairman, as fine a gentleman as ever graced Boston society.

Soon a Mr. Alcott rose and spoke as follows: "Mr. Chairman, I can tell this convention wherein you are all wrong, blind, and carnal. I am as pure and as wise as was Jesus Christ. The reason is, I eat nothing but pure vegetables. You eat cattle's flesh and sheep's flesh and fowl's flesh and swine's flesh. You are just what you eat: you are cattle and sheep and fowl and swine; you are ignorant and blind and carnal."

When the speaker had concluded I addressed the chair as follows :

"Mr. Chairman, with your permission I wish to ask the gentleman who has just taken his seat a question."

There were murmuring sounds in all parts of the house, and rap, rap, sounded the chairman's gavel, until silence was restored, when the chairman said : "Mr. Lee wishes to ask the last speaker a question. Proceed, Mr. Lee."

I proceeded by saying: "The speaker told us that we are just what we eat; that because we eat cattle's flesh and fowl's flesh and sheep's flesh and swine's flesh we are cattle and fowl and sheep and swine. He also told us that he eats nothing but vegetables. Now the question is, Does it not follow, by parity of reason, that he is a potato, a turnip, a pumpkin, or a squash ?"

The result can be imagined. Amid the racket was heard, in every part of the house, "Too much of the squash!"

Such episodes may have been of some use by relieving the mind for a moment from thoughts of sterner work and higher responsibilities ; but the work had to be performed, and the responsibilities had to be met, as the next chapter will show.

CHAPTER XXIV.

An Earnest Year's Work—Opposition on every Hand—
Discouraging Prospect.

IT has been seen that I commenced my labors in Massachusetts in November, 1839. I lectured at large through the State, and visited those places where labor was most needed. I made one tour down the cape during the winter, and found it very cold, yet winter is the best time to operate there. Most of the men follow the water, and are largely coasters and fishermen, and are from home during the summer, but all are at home during the winter. In this tour I was favored much with the company of the Rev. Frederick Upham, presiding elder. He was not only good company, but a good antislavery man, and I could get a hearing at some hour during his quarterly meetings. In one neighborhood I lectured in a Baptist church, and put up with the minister, who gave me the following item of his experience with the "Come-outers." It was on an exceeding cold winter's night, and he was sick and was taking a sweat under the administration of his daughter. He was seated in a chair covered with thick blankets, with a steaming arrangement under him, when a powerful rap was heard at the door. His daughter went to the door and found a person there who wished to see the elder. She told him he must come in, as the elder could not come to the door. No, he could not come in, but must see the elder at the door. She returned and told her father what the man said. She did not know him. He sent her back to tell the man he could not come to the door to see him, that he was taking a sweat, and if he wished to see him he must come in. He persisted that he could not come in, but that it was all-important that he should see him; that he had a message for him which he could deliver only in person, and at the door. The elder, thinking something very strange and important must be on hand, rose, blankets and all, and made his way to the door, and as he stuck his head out into the cold night air he recognized his neighbor, who said, "I have a message from God, which is, that you must repent or you will be damned," and he turned and away he went.

The elder felt as though he would like to shake him a little, but he was gone, and he felt that he was in too weak a condition to shake any one very severely, and so he returned quietly to his chair and finished his sweat.

I made one lecturing tour through the western part of the State. I gave a series of lectures in Westfield. At that time there was a large whip factory in this place in which whips were made by the thousand for the Southern market, for the express purpose of whipping slaves. Of course there was much opposition to abolitionism. I lectured in the Methodist church, and on going into the pulpit to deliver my second lecture I found one of the largest sized slave whips there. It was put there to remind me that I might get a touch of it if I continued my lectures. Not having the fear of slave whips before my eyes, I proceeded with my lecture, saying nothing about the whip. I spoke of the practice of tying slaves up and whipping them until they were bloody. At the right time I lifted the whip and cracked it nearly as loud as the report of a pistol, which made the people start, and I shouted at the same time, " That is the way they give it to them, and this is the instrument with which they do it, made here in Westfield. Will you ask again what we have to do with slavery here at the North?" I finished my course of lectures without getting whipped.

I made a summer tour down the cape, below where I went in my winter campaign, and spent some days at Provincetown, which is on the extreme point of the cape upon which old Ocean rolls his mad waves when the tempest is high. I found a very primitive yet noble-hearted people, antislavery almost to a man—and, I might add, woman. I made a tour through the northern portion of the State, where I met with the only attempt at personal violence in the whole State. In one locality a Congregational minister was notorious for his opposition to abolitionism.

15

Of course he, being a minister of the Gospel, would not cause or countenance any thing like a mob, yet when I had the courage to lecture within his parish we came near having a mob. There was no disturbance during the lecture, but when the meeting was dismissed the street in front of the building was found full of people. What they were there for could be known only by what they said and did. Some were heard to call for the lecturer, crying, "Where is he? Where is he? Catch him! Don't let him escape!" It was a dark night, and all the light there was came from the lamps which were still burning in the lecture hall, as the people were coming out, so that persons could be seen when in the door by those outside. As I appeared in the door an egg was thrown at my head with great force. There was a step down in coming out, and I stepped down just in time to escape the egg, it passing directly over my head, and a lady who was next behind me received the missile square on her nose, and she fell as quickly as she would if she had been shot through the head, though she was not very seriously injured. The moment I stepped out on one side of the door I was in the dark, and safe, with friends around me, and we walked quietly with the dispersing throng and reached my lodging. The next morning all was quiet and all well except the lady who got the egg which was intended for me, and she only had a nose a little swollen and sore, from which she soon recovered.

But the year drew to a close, and there fell upon our antislavery ranks discouragement, and a dark foreboding. There were more reasons than one for this, some of which I will name:

1. The division in the antislavery ranks weakened both sides.

2. The non-resistance, no-government, no-Church, no-Sabbath doctrine was so common and rampant among a class of antislavery men that the reputation of the whole suffered.

3. The political campaign of 1840 was disastrous to every thing good, and more especially to reforms which had to contend against popular sentiment, and make headway against the political tornado of log-cabins, hard cider, and coon skins. The like of this political fury was never seen before, and has never occurred since. I know what it was, for I stood in its focus, representing political antislavery, and boldly urged men to vote for James G. Birney for President of the United States. Of course, but little progress could be made, and only the most firm and uncompromising could be held under the concentrated contempt and scorn of Democrats and the denunciations, bluster, and wrath of Whigs; yet the tempest passed and left our Liberty Party intact as the nucleus for the rallying of a mighty power. Mr. Birney was not elected, for the same reason that Mr. Van Buren was not elected—neither got votes enough; and if we threw away our votes, the Democrats threw away their votes,

and the Whigs saved their votes, but to little purpose.

4. The financial disaster of the country was another cause of embarrassment to the antislavery cause. The issue between the Democrats and Whigs was a national bank or no national bank, and the Whigs labored to show that a sound currency could not be maintained with par value, in all parts of the country, without a national bank, and consequently ruin must be realized unless such a bank was chartered by Congress. Daniel Webster and Henry Clay had sounded the alarm in the United States Senate during the preceding session of Congress, and now it was the campaign cry and was echoed from every Whig political stump. This of itself was enough to produce a panic and financial ruin in a country where so much business was being conducted upon a credit system, and the ruin came. The Whigs took advantage of it and said, "We told you so." And, to turn it to account, they promised the working-classes two dollars a day and roast beef for dinner if they would vote the Whig ticket and secure a Whig administration. They succeeded, but the two dollars a day were slow in coming, and the roast beef was reserved for those who could afford to purchase and eat it. Nevertheless, the financial ruin nearly crushed the antislavery societies. Funds could not be raised as heretofore to pay agents, and it was under all these difficulties that I resigned my agency. Soon after my resignation the Society

was found to be bankrupt, and I secured a settlement by relinquishing more than half the amount due me, as a condition of receiving the balance, which certain persons taxed themselves to pay, there being no funds in the treasury. I had no plan for the future save one purpose, which was to fight rum, slavery, and the devil whatever betide.

CHAPTER XXV.

A Dark Day for Methodist Antislavery—Another Attempt to Rally—A Failure—My own Course the while—Secession.

THE close of 1840 was the darkest day to me, and, as I know, to many other ministers and members of the Methodist Episcopal Church who had made themselves prominent in the antislavery discussion. The fact was the tide turned against us. The pro-slavery powers of the Church had virtually triumphed, and were preparing to make an end of the contest by striking down the leaders. We knew it, we felt it, we looked it when we looked in each other's faces, while we said but little. For myself, I defied them in my heart, for, as a local preacher as I was, I could entrench myself in some antislavery Quarterly Conference, where they could get no judgment against me for antislavery. And if they could dislodge me by any process, the world outside of the Methodist Episcopal Church was large enough to hold me, if they could and should hurl me out, and there were pulpits enough open to me. But I was not the only one to suffer; there were many members and some ministers whom I had been instrumental in leading on in antislavery, until we had all reached what had become a precipice, from which we must start back, or go over; and I felt for others more than for myself; yet I said but little, and waited to see what would happen.

The Rev. Orange Scott, a member of the New England Conference, had been the acknowledged leader of the Methodist antislavery movement, and it was believed that he would be the first victim, and that a sufficient number of those who had stood by him in time past were now tired of the strife, and willing to give him up for the sake of peace and for restoration to the favor of the authorities of the Church and to their former positions.

Brother Scott had retired from active labor, and was residing at Newbury, Vt., on account of poor health. He wrote a few articles for the press about this time, in which he appeared to make some concessions, which I regarded as feelers, to learn, if possible, his security or insecurity in the Church. Not being satisfied with the state of things, he made one more effort to rally the antislavery forces in the Church. For this purpose he came to Lowell, Mass., where he had great strength, and organized a joint stock company for the purpose of publishing a weekly paper, to be called "The New England Christian Advocate." I had nothing to do with projecting the enterprise, or in organizing the association, but was invited to become the editor. As I was now out of employment I accepted.

It was too late; the old forces could not be rallied,

the paper was not sustained, and was discontinued at the end of the first volume.

I was not idle. In addition to editing the paper I preached as a supply in the First Methodist Episcopal Church in Lowell for a time, supplied vacant pulpits when called upon, and lectured on slavery and temperance anywhere and every-where I was invited, and usually had as much on hand as I could attend to.

During the winter I was urged by friends in Maine to visit that State for the purpose of making an argument before a committee of the legislature in support of petitions asking for antislavery action. I went, and not only addressed the committee of the legislature, but preached and lectured on slavery. When my work was done I started for home in the stage, leaving Augusta at four o'clock P. M. The weather was colder than I had ever seen before. At ten o'clock the stage stopped for the night, but at four A. M. we started again, and were to reach Portland, the terminus of the railroad, to take the eight o'clock train for Boston. It was the coldest ride I ever enjoyed, or, rather, endured. It appeared as though I must perish. The stage was a few moments behind time, and we had to jump from the stage into the car, and away we went. There was a red-hot stove in the car, and then for the first time I appreciated the blessedness of railroad travel in cold weather.

On my arrival home I learned that the temperance society had invited all the ministers of Lowell to preach a sermon before the society in the City Hall, and that the ministers had held a meeting, accepted, and divided the work, assigning a particular subject to each minister. They had assigned to me the subject of Prohibitory Law. I was ripe on that subject, having advocated prohibition in some newspaper articles I wrote for the press in 1836. This, however, was not known in Lowell.

When my turn came I delivered my sermon to an immense crowd, his Honor the Mayor presiding. In it, I believe, I vindicated the right and necessity of prohibiting the traffic in intoxicating drinks by penal law. It was published, and I believe was the first of the kind published in this country.

When "The New England Christian Advocate" was discontinued, the association left the subscription list in my hands, and I availed myself of it by issuing a semi-monthly, entitled "The Sword of Truth." This was not intended to be distinctly antislavery, but was intended to oppose some wild theological views springing up, and to defend orthodox views. The opposers of antislavery would not take it because it belonged to a notorious abolitionist, and many of the antislavery Methodists would not take it because it did not oppose slavery as the "Advocate" had done. This left me only the support of the few orthodox people outside of the Methodist Episcopal Church who would patronize my enterprise, and I soon discontinued the "Sword."

There was an unoccupied Methodist Episcopal Church in Andover. They had been regularly supplied from the Conference, but, owing to their extreme antislavery views and the want of sufficient support, they were left without a pastor. They invited me to preach to them, and I did so, and removed to Andover in the autumn of 1842. While I supplied the church on the Sabbath, I went out and lectured wherever there was a call, and kept up my war against slavery.

It was during this period that what was called the new science of mesmerism found its way into Andover, and for a time produced much excitement. I investigated the subject until I believed that I understood it as well as any of the operators, and could do as much with it as the best of them, and then I abandoned it forever. Not because I believed it was sinful in itself, but for the reason that I believed that no man could practice it as a profession, nor even frequently and publicly, without impairing his ministerial reputation. Whatever he may do, or however honestly he may do it, the incredulity of many will cause them to believe him to be an impostor, and his reputation will be damaged. I felt I had not finished the work which God had given me to do, and dared not to put my reputation at hazard.

Soon after this there came one of the traveling operators in mesmerism, and gave out that he would perform in a public hall. I went to the entertainment and saw a number of the students from the theological school present who knew me and my relation to the subject. The lecturer remarked that it was through the mesmeric power that Christ performed all his miracles, and that if he was as perfect as Christ was he could do as great miracles as Christ did. When he had concluded he invited any one to ask any questions. I saw the students all look at me, which I understood to mean, "Will you let that pass?" I rose and inquired if I understood him aright, and got him to repeat his words, and then stated that I could see no tendency in the power he displayed to produce a miracle if that power was increased to any extent. "Christ fed five thousand. Now if you can feed one person, or partially feed one person, I will admit that the same power in kind might feed five thousand if sufficiently increased."

"That is all plain," he answered; "I can put a person into the mesmeric state and cause him to think that he eats, and he will be satisfied."

I rejoined, "Suppose I allow all that, I must inquire how many baskets' full you will have left?" If he had unexpectedly been struck by the current of a galvanic battery he would not have been more astonished.

All this time the prospects of the earnest, outspoken ministers and people in the Methodist Episcopal Church grew darker and darker, and while all thought much and asked each other what the next move would be, and what the end of these things would be, no one could tell. The actual state of things will be described in a future chapter. It was in this darkest and most sullenly silent hour that had held the murky atmosphere in abeyance for years that the bomb of secession was exploded.

CHAPTER XXVI.

The First Secession Trumpet-blast—It Fell upon My own
Ears with Startling Surprise—My own Position Unknown
—A Letter from the Boston Preachers' Meeting on the Sub-
ject—The Reason why I was not Consulted.

IN October, 1842, Rev. Orange Scott held a private
meeting with a few confidential friends, in which
it was agreed to secede from the Methodist Episcopal
Church and organize a new Church upon antislavery
principles to be called "The Wesleyan Methodist
Connection of America." The first that I knew of
this movement was through the press. I wondered,
as I had cause, why I was not consulted; but there
was a reason which will soon appear. The facts
which are about to be given show that neither party
knew what my views were in regard to secession, and
what my course would be.

The publication of Brother Scott's plan of secession
produced an excitement among all classes. The
Preachers' Meeting of Boston caused one of their
number to write to me a letter in the following
words:

If your principles and convictions of right will allow you
to do so, I know what I say when I tell you that you shall
have any position in the Church you desire if you will come
out and wield your vigorous pen against secession.

The above letter reached me before I met or heard from Brother Scott, and I answered it the same hour it was received by simply saying that Luther Lee was not in the market.

When I met Brother Scott I demanded of him why he did not consult me in regard to that meeting and let me take part in its deliberations. He looked me square in my eyes, like an honest man, as he was, and said: "I was afraid of you; I did not know that you would agree with me, and I knew if you did not, and I consulted you, you would sound the alarm before I could get my document before the people, and forestall and greatly embarrass my movement. I wanted to get my document before the people before they heard of it from any other source."

I had no plan matured for my future course when the secession document reached me. I was waiting to see what would come to pass. I felt that the time was near when justice to myself, to the Methodist Episcopal Church, to God and the world, would require me to assume some position different from that which I occupied. During those dark days, when every body must have known I was not satisfied with my position, I was offered a position and a pulpit in other denominations; but I was a Methodist, and I knew I was a Methodist from the deep and honest convictions of my heart. I also knew that those who reached out to me a kind, Christian hand were not Methodists, though good Christian people. I therefore held myself in a very unsatisfactory and uncomfortable position. When I heard the trump of secession it impressed me with the idea that the organization of a new connection, thoroughly Methodistic and thoroughly antislavery, would, in the circumstances, best promote the glory and truth of God and the cause of humanity, and place me in a better position to do the work to which I believed God had called me. Had I known all that would follow, which is not allowed to mortals, I might have decided upon another course than that I pursued, and yet I cannot say that I should. I had full confidence in the Boston brethren, and believed that they would fulfill their promise to the utmost of their ability if I pursued the course they suggested; but in view of all the efforts which had been made to crush antislavery out of the Church, for me to draw my sword in opposition to secession would be to justify church fellowship with slave-holders, and look like an attempt to drive back into such fellowship those who were attempting to escape from it. So deep was my conviction that slavery was "the sum of all villainies" that I shrunk from such a position as a living man would shrink from the touch of death. So things appeared to me when looking at them from my own standpoint. Others, looking at them from another standpoint, saw them differently. I resolved to go with the secessionists, and with me to resolve was always to act, and at once I withdrew from the Methodist

Episcopal Church, assigning my reasons in a printed document.

The full reasons which I believed justified secession must be given hereafter, but it is necessary to remark here that in going with the secessionists I did not then, and do not now, hold myself responsible for the motives that controlled all seceders; but I was then, and am now, responsible for the act of secession and for the motives which led me to perform that act. Of course myself and others were severely censured and our motives were impugned. Ever since my return to the Methodist Episcopal Church some of the older members of the Detroit Conference have attempted to convince me that my act of seceding was wrong. Such persons have no conception of the real facts in the case, as they were then and are still seen by me; and in giving my reasons for secession I shall simply state the facts as they appeared to me, seen from my stand-point. Without such statement my book would not be a truthful, faithful autobiography.

CHAPTER XXVII.

Reasons which I believed Justified Secession from the Methodist Episcopal Church.

WHEN I entered upon my antislavery work I had not the shadow of a thought of ever leaving the Methodist Episcopal Church. I loved her and was ardently devoted to her interests, as my entire past life testified. My only object was to purify her from the crime and corruption of slavery, and I believe the same to have been true of all the early leading antislavery ministers in the Church. Of course we did not understand the herculean work we undertook. It was probably for the best that we did not understand the matter. As we proceeded light was evolved, unknown facts came to light, and new facts transpired, and we saw more and more the difficulties of freeing the Church from slavery, so long as slave-holding existed in the State. The weight of evidence seemed to be against success, and we appeared defeated in the object we set out to secure ; and it was natural to review and sum up what had been done and inquire what more could be done ; and here follows a statement of the facts as I found them, summing up from my stand-point.

I. I believed, I knew, that slavery was a great evil,

16

a sin against God and man—so bad, so corrupt and corrupting in its influence, as to be incapable of cure or of essentially relieving modification. It is too late to require proof of this fact.

II. The Methodist Episcopal Church appeared to indorse, and to be determined to defend and maintain, slavery as it existed in the Church, while I was unable to see any essential moral difference between slavery in the Church and slavery out of the Church. Of this statement there appeared to me the most conclusive evidence, and, as it is a fundamental fact, a brief outline of the proof is given.

1. Ministers were allowed, without rebuke from the authorities of the Church, to advocate slavery as morally right, as indorsed in the Scriptures, as a divine institution; and this some did in their pulpits, in Annual Conferences, in General Conference, and in public discussions. The facts are on record elsewhere.

2. Ministers were not allowed to condemn slavery as a sin in their pulpits or out of their pulpits without censure. The General Conference advised all wholly to refrain, and Annual Conferences construed that advice as law; so that every minister that preached a sermon against slavery, or declared in public his belief that slavery was a sin, was judged to be contumacious and insubordinate; and men were tried and condemned just on such charges, based upon such facts, as in the cases of True, Floy, and others in the

New York Conference, and many others in different localities.

3. The Bishops presiding in Annual Conferences put resolutions to vote justifying slavery and condemning abolition, but refused to put any resolution to vote in an Annual Conference condemning slavery as a sin. These facts are recorded elsewhere, and have become matters of history.

4. The General Conference of 1836, by resolution, condemned, unheard, two of its members on a report that they had attended and spoken at an abolition meeting, while it refused to censure slavery.

5. The General Conference of 1840 censured, by vote, New Hampshire, New England, and Oneida Annual Conferences for their action against slavery, while it laid upon the table an amendment to include in the censure the Georgia Conference for equally decisive action in favor of slavery. Other Annual Conferences acted in favor of slavery, of which no notice was ever taken.

6. The General Conference of 1840 adopted what is known as the colored testimony resolution, which was undeniably in the interest of slavery, and was antichristian, and not to be justified on any moral ground. This involved the whole Church in the disgrace and guilt of denying to a class of Christians the rights of membership in the Church.

7. While the Church allowed both ministers and members to hold slaves, and intended to continue to

do so, she waged what was intended to be an exterminating war upon abolitionism and abolitionists, intending to silence both, or drive them out of the Church. Of this there was not a shadow of doubt.

8. All the official organs of the Church took sides in favor of slavery as it existed in the Church, and against antislavery and antislavery men, attacking their characters, impugning their motives, and descendng to a low blackguarding of them. In this course the "Christian Advocate and Journal," of New York city, took the lead. Of my humble self, of whom it said as good things as it ever said of any man, it now, for no other reason than that I opposed slavery, attacked me, representing me as the enemy of the Church, unworthy of a place in her pulpits, and did all it could to destroy my influence, and went so far and let itself down so low as to say I was "a metaphysical tadpole, always wiggling to stir up the muddy waters of strife."

9. The administrators of the Church pursued a persistent course of opposition and oppression toward antislavery ministers and Churches. This is true of Bishops and presiding elders. Presiding elders were removed from their districts because they would not pledge themselves to keep silent on the subject of slavery. Preachers were sent to poor charges, and strong antislavery Churches had pro-slavery preachers sent to them to annoy and wear them out. These facts are on record and have become history. In one

case a strong antislavery Church requested the Bishop to send them a man they named. The Bishop refused. They then asked him to send them any one of five they named, and he refused. They then asked him to leave them without a pastor, and he refused that. They then asked him not to send them a particular man they named; they would receive any other preacher he saw fit to send them save that one, who was offensive to them; and the Bishop sent them that man. They refused to let him into their pulpit, for which the preacher, by a published manifesto, declared them all expelled *en masse*. The Church denied his right to do so, and appealed from his authority to the next Conference, in which another Bishop presided, who decided in favor of the legality of the preacher's act, and against the Church, adding, as a comment, " There is energy in Methodism

All these transactions convinced me and others that the authorities of the Methodist Episcopal Church intended to support slavery as it existed in the Church, and to drive antislavery and antislavery men out of it.

III. The course pursued by the authorities of the Church, as has been set forth, and as might be set forth in greater numbers of cases and in fuller detail, had crippled the antislavery cause in the Church.

The best, strongest, and most active antislavery

preachers, being made the principal objects of all these assaults and proscriptions, were damaged in their reputations and shorn of their prestige and influence.

Many of the weaker sort, who were bold when there was no danger, were unable to breast the storm, and ceased to act with the antislavery party, by which the abolitionists were cut down in their number of votes in the Conference.

Numbers got tired of the contest with the authorities of the Church and of the proscription it brought upon them, and went over to the other side, some of whom confessed that they were governed by the " bread-and-butter argument " in so doing.

The aspect now was very dark. Some of the authorities boasted that antislavery was subdued in the Church, and the belief was common that there was not strength enough to protect the leaders, and that they would be stricken down at the next session of the Conference. It was whispered that Orange Scott would be the first victim, and it was believed by many. There appeared but one alternative, either to submit and take the ecclesiastical gag, or be ostracised. Some had already closed their lips who had been wont to speak for the dumb. That I could not do. I could not remain any longer in a slave-holding Church, where I was not free to oppose such a damning sin as slavery, and I seceded.

CHAPTER XXVIII.

The Utica Convention — Organization of the Wesleyan Methodist Connection of America.

THE paper which contained the secession procla- mation also contained a call for a convention to assemble at Utica, N. Y., May 31, 1843, for the pur- pose of organizing the proposed new Church. I knew enough of human nature to know that there would be a want of harmony in the convention, and that it would be difficult to unite all parties on all the questions involved in Church government. Hav- ing given in my adhesion to the measure, I went to the convention determined to secure an organization, and to get as good a one as possible. I went pre- pared to make great sacrifices of my personal views, if necessary, to secure an organization, trusting to the future to improve it. There were extreme views. Rev. E. Smith, from the West, was inclined to High- Church notions. Brother Scott, who was the ac- knowledged leader of the movement, and who was unanimously elected president of the convention, was in favor of an episcopacy, with limited and well- guarded powers. Some were congregational in their views, and were for absolute independence, making each congregation absolutely independent of all be-

yond. I soon became convinced that neither extreme
could be carried out, and struck for a medium ground,
and that was the kind of organization which was
finally adopted. I soon became convinced that my
moderate views must prevail, or we could get no organization, for nothing else could command a majority, and soon had the satisfaction of seeing them
adopted, and thought the danger over. Alas, how
mistaken was I!

An unexpected element of discord was introduced
by the Rev. Edward Smith, from Pittsburgh, which
he was determined to force into the Discipline. It
was a rule excluding all members of secret societies
from the Church. Smith was a man of great power,
and had as strong a will as any man I ever knew, and,
of course, he rallied a party, whom he held in his
strong hand.

Orange Scott, Jotham Horton, and LaRoy Sunderland were Masons, and, being strong men, had their
party, and steel met steel, and for a time it really
looked as though the convention would break up without effecting an organization, or divide and result in
two organizations, which would be fatal to success,
and which I resolved to prevent if possible. Fortunately for my purpose, no man in the convention
knew what my views were on the subject. I was a
Mason, but did not feel myself under any masonic
obligation to make myself its champion on that occasion, as all true Masons know I was not. This fact

borne in mind will throw some light on my after conduct. While the debate and excitement raged I lay low, reserving what strength I had for the crisis, which I saw would soon come. A point was reached where it was seen that Smith could not command a majority for his extreme and proscriptive rule, and he declared that he and his friends would withdraw from the convention, and take no further part in its proceedings. This I knew would be fatal, and felt that my time for action had come, for which I was prepared. To meet that crisis I had carefully drawn a compromise rule, which was not law, but which simply advised our people not to join secret societies. This I offered as a compromise, and enforced it by the best speech I was capable of making. My extreme solicitude to secure an organization enabled me to throw some pathos into my effort, and by shedding a few tears—some others shed tears because I did—my rule was adopted by a handsome majority. Scott, Horton, and Sunderland did not like it; they wanted nothing said on the subject; but they accepted of it in good faith as a compromise, and as the best thing that could be obtained in the circumstances. Smith frowned darkly, and would have bolted had not the compromise swept away from him so many of his supporters that he could not bolt with any show of strength, and he held on and reserved himself for a future occasion, as will be seen.

The Discipline being completed, the convention proceeded to divide the territory in which we had any show of strength into Annual Conferences, and appointing a president *pro tem.* for each. In each Conference all the charges that were represented or reported were supplied by appointing such preachers to them as reported themselves, or as were reported as ready for work. In this there was much uncertainty for want of reliable information, as was learned when the several Conferences met in their first sessions. I was appointed president of the New York Conference, and stationed at Syracuse. The work of the convention being finished it adjourned *sine die*, and each man hastened to his post or field of labor. In view of the haste in which the business of the convention was done, and the uncertainty of the results which might follow, the first General Conference was appointed to assemble in Cleveland in October, 1844, only about one year and a half after the convention.

CHAPTER XXIX.

The Effect of the Wesleyan Organization upon the Methodist Episcopal Church — How their Action Affected the New Movement—My personal Efforts.

THE policy of the Methodist Episcopal Church was at once changed on the announcement of the secession plan. Between the issuing of the call and the meeting of the convention arrangements were made for holding three Methodist Episcopal conventions in New England—one in Boston, one in Hallowell, Me., and one in Claremont, N. H. The Bishops, who had refused to put to vote any resolution in the Annual Conferences which declared slave-holding a sin, now allowed them to adopt such resolutions without obstruction. All were free to talk against slavery; lips which had always been closed, or opened only to execrate abolition and traduce abolitionists, were now opened wide to denounce slavery, and one wild anti-slavery shout was heard, which nearly drowned the vociferations of the few seceders. This course, no doubt, very much crippled the Wesleyan movement, and prevented many from seceding from the Methodist Episcopal Church who would otherwise have done so. It furnished an excuse for some who had been longing for deliverance from pro-slavery pro-

scription, yet loved the loaves and fishes which seceders had to leave behind them. Many honest men, yet
superficial thinkers, believed there was now no good
reason for seceding, as they were free to oppose slavery in the Church. But for this stroke of policy the
new movement would have swept New England, and
become strong in other parts of the country. As it
was, it made a good fight for a few years.

From the convention I hastened home, and, as soon
as possible, I removed with my family from Andover,
Mass., to Syracuse, N. Y., to which I had been appointed by the convention. This appointment was
but little more than nominal, as the arrangement was
first made between me and a delegation from Syracuse to the convention. On reaching Syracuse I
found a small band of seceders, but no place of worship, and I held forth on the first Sabbath in the
Congregational church, which was offered for me and
my people.

My friends secured a hall as a place of worship, and
I went to work in earnest, in the face of great opposition from the Methodist Episcopal Church, as my
membership were nearly all seceders from them, and
as new ones occasionally left them and came over to
us. My Church was neither numerous nor wealthy,
but a truer company of men and women never
breathed. I had frequent calls to visit other places
to preach and lecture, and in the course of the year
I organized a number of Wesleyan Churches. I

also wrote constantly for the "True Wesleyan," a weekly paper published by Brother Scott, and which became the organ of the Wesleyan Connection. I was abundant in labors, preaching more, lecturing more, and writing more, than any other man in the field. When I commenced my labors in Syracuse, the Unitarian society was building a new house of worship, and when it was finished my Church secured the one they vacated, which greatly enlarged my opportunity to do good, and build up a Church and congregation.

In the autumn of 1843 a messenger was sent to me from Jamestown, Chautauqua County, in the western part of the State, who told me the following story: He was a principal member of the Methodist Episcopal Church in Jamestown. A musical instrument had been introduced into the church, to which some were opposed, of whom he was one. While the members were discussing the question preparatory for a final vote, whether the instrument should remain in the church or be removed, the preacher in charge came in and removed it *vi et armis*, and refused to allow them to vote on the question, saying he had an absolute right to control the music, and that they had no voice in the matter. The exercise of such power was worse to him than the instrument of music, and the two parties united to contest the question with the preacher, and carried it to the Quarterly Conference. The presiding elder decided that the preacher was right, and would not allow an appeal to the body. They then appealed to the Annual Conference, and the Bishop decided that the preacher and presiding elder were right. During this contest the preacher had been very overbearing and insulting in his language, and they felt that they could not submit to it, but did not know what they could do to relieve themselves.

At that stage of things a local preacher from a distance visited the place, and learning their condition, asked them why they did not go to the Wesleyans? But who were they? They did not know that there were any such people. He could tell them but little about the Wesleyans, but said there was a preacher in Syracuse, by the name of Luther Lee, who, if they would write to him, would give them all necessary information.

They were too much in earnest to trust to letters, and sent their leading man to see me. I explained to him our origin, our principles, and our church government. It was all right, except our antislavery; they were not antislavery, and he did not know how they would bear that. I told him I could do nothing for them unless they would accept of our antislavery; it was our rallying-cry.

He concluded to try it, and engaged me to visit them at a future day agreed upon, and he promised to make arrangements for me to lecture at different points in the vicinity, as I judged it would not pay to make so long a journey to address one congregation. He assured me there were some persons of his acquaintance into whose hands he could put that matter who would take pleasure in making arrangements for any number of lectures. I gave him our Discipline, and dismissed him with my blessing. The result of my visit will be given in the next chapter.

CHAPTER XXX.

ON arriving at Jamestown I learned that several appointments had been made for me to lecture on the subject of slavery. There were a few anti-slavery men scattered through the county, but as it was a border county but little had been done, and they were ready to rally on learning that a foreign lecturer was among them. The campaign was under the charge of a Mr. Broadhead, a local preacher of much ability. He had traveled under the presiding elder, and knew the country and the people.

I commenced in Jamestown, and as I had been informed that those who had sent for me were not anti-slavery, I had sense and policy enough to make my first lecture an *exposé* of the wickedness of slavery. I did what I could to lift the vail from its horrid features, and expose its cruelty, corruption, and damning guilt. When I had concluded I have no doubt every hearer was opposed to slavery in the abstract, and I left the discussion of its relation to the North and the Church for the future, and proceeded to fulfill the appointments that had been made elsewhere. I had one appointment to lecture of an afternoon in the Congregational church in Salem, on the Lake Shore Road. When I arrived and had entered the pulpit, Brother Broadhead, who was with me, whispered, and told me there were a dozen or more Methodist Episcopal preachers in the congregation. I knew enough about Methodist preachers to be aware that if a dozen of them had got together to hear me lecture, it meant business, and I resolved to make the most of my first chance. If they had come to attack me, as I believed, I determined to give a good excuse for making their assault. I attacked the pro-slavery position of the Methodist Episcopal Church, and recited her pro-slavery action, and showed up the arbitrary and oppressive measures resorted to by the authorities of the Church to crush abolitionists. These statements, though literally true, were unknown to my clerical hearers, and they regarded them as abolition slanders.

By the time I had finished my lecture they were lashed into fury, and before I had time to sit down they were all clamoring for a hearing. I had blown off my effervescence, was quite cool, and said, " One at a time, gentlemen, and you will be better understood." This had a calming influence, and one spoke for the whole, and charged me with having slandered the Church, and challenged me for a public discussion of the questions in issue.

I told them I had an engagement for every day until I should be compelled to return home, yet I

17

would accept their challenge if we could agree on proper terms of debate and the time of meeting. So anxious were they for a discussion that I had no difficulty in obtaining fair terms. It was agreed that we should meet in that church where we were in four weeks from that time.

Two questions were to be discussed :

1. Does the Methodist Episcopal Church justify slavery ?

2. Is the government of the Methodist Episcopal Church arbitrary and unscriptural ?

It was agreed that each party should speak thirty minutes alternately. They were left free to bring who or as many as they pleased.

It was agreed that they should choose one man and I one, and they two should choose a third, and that the three should preside and keep order, and decide all questions of order, but should not decide the main questions.

At the time agreed upon we met and opened the debate in the Congregational house where the challenge was given, but we soon found it was too small. The Methodists had a large house near by, and an effort was made to obtain it ; but the trustees refused to open it for the debate. This was thought to be illiberal, as their preachers had given the challenge. The Baptists had a large house about two miles away, on the main road, which they offered, and we went to that.

My opponents were Rev. J. J. Steadman, presiding elder of Jamestown District; Rev. Professor Calvin Kingsley, of Alleghany College; and Rev. Thomas Graham, from some charge within the district—three against one. I had half the time, but had to talk as much as the three. But I had the advantage, for I was an experienced debater. I understood the subject better than they did, and, in the main, I had the right side.

I had the affirmative, and very soon put them on the defense and gave them as much work as they knew how to attend to.

On the first question, " Does the Methodist Episcopal Church justify slavery ?" I opened with the undeniable fact that it was a slave-holding Church ; that there were hundreds of slave-holding preachers and thousands of slave-holding members. I insisted that slavery existed in the Church, and it made no effort to get it out, but opposed every effort that was made to get it out, and did all that could be done to suppress the discussion of its wrong. If the Church did not justify slavery she did not justify her own conduct. If the Church did not justify slavery she did not justify the conduct of her ministers and members, and did not justify what she allowed. Slavery is right or wrong, and if the Church does not justify it as right she must condemn it as wrong ; and she proclaims her ministers and members wrong-doers, and herself a wrong-doer, for allowing ministers and members to practice wrong without disciplining them for their wrong deeds.

This argument had great power with a popular audience, and my opponents found it difficult to struggle against it.

I supported my argument further by quoting and urging the principal facts of the terrible war which the Church had waged against the abolitionists, expelling members and deposing ministers for their opposition to slavery. Numbers of clear cases were stated, and names, places, and dates given.

Pro-slavery resolutions were cited passed by slaveholding Conferences, while Conferences were not allowed to resolve that slave-holding is a sin.

The advocacy of slavery as a biblical and divine institution by prominent ministers was appealed to as proof that the Church justified slavery. They had done it without rebuke, while the highest authority of the Church had condemned abolitionism without qualification, and condemned ministers in the same unqualified language for attending an abolition meeting.

The pro-slavery action of the General Conference was cited and applied with force. The colored-testimony resolution, so-called, adopted by the General Conference in 1844, was urged as proof. This resolution condemned the act of allowing colored members of the Church, however pious and truthful, to testify in a Church trial against a white man.

The second question, " Is the government of the Methodist Episcopal Church arbitrary and unscriptural ?" was argued with equal earnestness.

The first part of the question was soon disposed of by me. That is arbitrary which depends upon the will of one man. The Bishops of the Methodist Episcopal Church have the power to appoint every traveling preacher to his field of labor, and is under no constitutional or statutory obligation to consult the preacher or the Church to which he is sent. Nothing could be more arbitrary. I was under no obligation to prove that a thing is wrong because it is arbitrary ; it is only the fact, and that cannot be denied, yet cases of its abuse were cited.

On the second part of the question I rested my argument mainly upon two facts, for which I contended sharply. The first was that the apostolic Churches were independent, self-governing bodies, and that the Methodist Episcopal Church excludes the laity from all voice in the rule-making power of the Church, which was then a fact. The above is a meager outline. The debate took a wide range, and was continued three days and evenings. Many side issues were contested. One episode is worthy of notice.

When I introduced the colored-testimony resolution my opponents denied that any such resolution was adopted by the General Conference. I re-affirmed my statement very positively, and they denied it again as positively as I affirmed. I knew they were mistaken, but could say nothing to convince them, they were so certain that they were right. This placed me at a disadvantage, for it was the word of one against three. I felt stung, and, with an impressive earnestness, affirmed that I was right, and that if God let me live I would in due time appear in that community with the documents, and prove the truth of what I affirmed.

My opponents unwisely attempted to make a little capital out of my predicament, and said I had no business there without the documents; that they had all the documents they needed.

At once I demanded that they produce the documents. Up to this point, I have no doubt, they believed they were right, but the confidence with which I demanded the documents shook their faith in themselves, and they refused to produce them. I appealed to the presiding board, and they decided that they were bound to produce them, and they presented a file of the official organ of the Church, in which the proceedings of the General Conference were published. I was so familiar with the whole proceedings that it took me but a moment to select the right number, and to find the right paragraph, and I read the matter just as I had affirmed. This was very damaging to them, but I was content to be vindicated without making any further words over the matter.

When the debate closed some of the people were

urgent to have it put to the vote of the assembly. They opposed it, and I supported them so far as to say that no provision had been made in the contract for a vote, and that neither party had any right to demand a vote. The moderators wisely refused to put it to a vote, but the people had become excited, and the moment the debate was declared closed one man put the vote, and it was carried in my favor with a general shout.

At the close my opponents challenged me to renew the debate with them in four weeks at Jamestown, which was the objective point of my first visit, and I accepted. Why they wished to renew the debate at that point I could not understand, unless they supposed they had lost the argument because I was so much better prepared for the discussion than they, which I certainly was, and that they believed they could recover themselves and their cause by renewing it after they should have made thorough preparation.

CHAPTER XXXI.

The Second Debate — The Result — The Organization of a Wesleyan Church at Jamestown.

IN the first discussion I found it physically hard work to speak against three opponents, being compelled to speak three times as much as one of them, and secured the assistance of the Rev. Edward Smith for the second debate. Mr. Smith was a man of superior ability and a very able debater. His logic may not have been quite as sharp-cornered as mine, but it was round and full; and though he had not so great power of condensation, it taking him longer to elaborate an argument, when he reached his conclusion it was sure to be irresistible, if he had the right side of the question.

I found my opponents had made elaborate preparation, and had come prepared to discuss, not only the main but all side issues. As the debate took the same general course as in the first discussion but little need be reported here beyond a few new points.

When we bore down on the pro-slavery character of the Church Mr. Kingsley defended her on the ground that she occupied an apostolic position, that slavery existed in the apostolic Church, under the eyes of Peter and Paul. In proof of this he quoted certain scriptures, and, being a scholar, he read from Roman history in Latin and translated it as he read. This was to prove that slavery existed in the Roman empire in the time of Paul and Peter. It was insisted that this must determine the meaning of those scriptures which appear to refer to slavery. This argument occupied more than thirty minutes, and I made no reply to it until it was finished. I then replied upon two grounds:

1. Paul gave authoritative directions which would have extirpated slavery if it existed in the Church.

2. The question is not, Did slavery exist in the apostolic Church? nor Is slavery right or wrong as it exists in the Methodist Episcopal Church? but Does the Methodist Episcopal Church justify slavery? My opponent, in trying to prove that slavery in the Church has apostolic sanction, virtually admits that the Church does justify it, and thus he gives up the argument. He may take which horn of the dilemma he pleases: he may say the Church does justify slavery, and thereby concede the question; or he may persist in denying that the Church justifies slavery, and thereby admit that the Church condemns what he claims to have proved Paul and Peter justified.

My reply was like the explosion of a shell in the center of their citadel, and they could do but little more than to defend the position of the Church, rather than proving that she does not justify slavery, which the question required them to do.

They often became personal in the latter part of the debate, and often resorted to ridicule. While I never made such attacks I did not intend to allow my opponents to make any capital out them at my expense, and often repelled them with a severe repartee, one instance of which I will give. If it amuses the reader as much as it did the audience it will pay. These sallies were most frequently made by Mr. Graham, who prided himself upon his logic and his wit. He attacked one of the best arguments of my Brother Smith, ridiculed it, and finally said he could not see what his opponent put forth such an argument for, unless it was as a cabbage-leaf that he might stick his head under it and get out of sight.

Brother Smith was a native Virginian, with a very large head, covered with a profusion of gray hair, standing up endwise. I replied by calling attention to the fact that ridicule is not argument, and that good debaters never resort to it while they have good arguments to offer. I then quoted Mr. Graham's words and, pointing to Smith, said, "Those gray hairs are not so dishonorable as to need covering with a cabbage-leaf, and it may be doubted if cabbage-leaves grow large enough in this north country to cover that great head;" and then, pointing to Graham, said, "A cabbage-leaf might cover the head of my friend on the other side, for nothing can be more in accordance with nature than that a cabbage-leaf should be fitted in size to the head upon which it grows."

Professor Kingsley, who appeared to enjoy the sally, picked up a book and commenced measuring Graham's head. The assembly was convulsed.

This second debate was continued through three days and three evenings. The hard-fought battle was ended, and of the result I need only say, that I organized a Wesleyan Church, into which nearly all the members of the Methodist Episcopal Church entered —I believe all the male members except one. Two of my opponents I have never seen since. They have both been some time dead. I met Professor Kingsley afterward, and we became warm friends. He became a strong antislavery member of the General Conference, and was elected Bishop. He has gone to his reward, and I yet linger upon earth.

CHAPTER XXXII.

The First Session of the New York Conference—An Omnium Gatherum—Elected President—Appointed Conference Missionary—Elected a Delegate to the General Conference.

THE Conference was organized upon paper at the Utica convention, and I was appointed provisional president, to act until the Conference should hold its first session and elect a president. The place determined upon was Syracuse, and was in the spring of 1844. My provisional presidency imposed upon me the duty of presiding until the Conference could come to a vote and elect a president, which was not so easily done as might be supposed. At the time and place appointed for the Conference there was a gathering, but it was an *omnium gatherum*. There were a few persons who were undoubtedly entitled to seats, and who had sufficient experience to do business orderly and correctly; but a large number were persons who had been roused by the new movement and jumped upon the moving car to be carried into a position of prosperity and fame they knew not where nor how. They had no knowledge of conference matters, and they came to teach, and could talk, and thought they were Solons or Solomons of a new and great Church. We had no reliable record to appeal to. It was found that the list of preachers and appointments derived from the Utica convention could not be depended upon. There were some worthy preachers and reliable charges in that list, but others were mere myths. The whole thing had to be sifted, and finally a roll was made out, the best we could do. The Conference went into an election, and I was elected president. I was also elected a delegate to the General Conference.

The Conference proceeded with its business; some were received on trial and some were elected to elders' orders and ordained. A committee elected by the Conference, of which I was chairman by virtue of my office as president, made the appointments for the year. My case was disposed of by the Conference, which appointed me by vote a Conference missionary, to travel at large and preach and lecture and organize Churches. The work being accomplished, the Conference adjourned, and each man went his way. My mission required that I should have a horse and carriage, and as soon as I could purchase I was in the field.

When autumn approached I made my arrangements to attend the General Conference, which was to assemble at Cleveland, Ohio, the first of October. My father-in-law years before had removed to Ohio, and on visiting the East the fall before took with him my second son, a lad in his fourteenth year, with the understanding that we should visit them and

bring him home at the time of the General Conference.   In accordance with this plan I started with
my wife to make a lecturing and missionary tour in
the western part of the State, and at the right time
cross Pennsylvania into Ohio and make our visit and
attend the General Conference.   In prosecuting this
plan we reached Jamestown, my old battle-ground,
where we were intercepted by a letter informing us
of the death of our son in Ohio.   It was a severe
blow, but we had both learned and confessed before
this that God reigns and governs all things well.
After spending a short time with sympathizing
friends in Jamestown, we passed on and made our
visit, and attended the General Conference.

CHAPTER XXXIII.

The First Wesleyan General Conference—Elected President
—The Secret-society Question—On the Verge of an Explosion—Elected Editor—Homeward Bound—A Terrible Storm.

WHEN the General Conference assembled, Orange
Scott was elected president on the first ballot,
but declined. On a second ballot I was elected. I
expected a stormy time, yet I accepted and took the
chair, and the Conference proceeded to business.
While appointing the standing committees a motion
was made to appoint a committee on secret societies.
This waked up the disturbing element which came so
near breaking us up in the Utica convention. I
dreaded it as much as I would a tornado, and I soon
found I had one on hand. It was not yet known
where I stood, which, I believe, was fortunate, otherwise I do not believe I could have held the Conference in the struggle. The committee was ordered
amid much excitement, and the vote indicated that
the anti-secret society men had a small majority.

The committee in due time reported a rule excluding the members of all secret societies from the Church.
It was urged by Smith, Walker, and others, and opposed by Scott, Horton, and others. Scott and Horton
were cool debaters, but Smith was all fire and flame

on this subject. Had the question been on the admission of the devil into the Church he could not have been more furious. He could not wait to reply to Scott's arguments; he denounced them and the man that advanced them, and I had to call him to order. This only roused the lion in him still more, and, looking terribly at me, he declared he would not come to order; and I do not know but some of the timid ones expected to see me swallowed whole, as he was a very large and powerful man. I faced him sternly and said, "You will come to order if there's power enough in this house to bring you to order." This brought a crisis, for a large portion of the house rose to their feet and affirmed, "The chair shall be sustained."

Brother Smith cooled down and said, "I will come to order, and if the chair will overlook my offense and allow me to proceed, I will proceed in order." I replied, "The member from Pittsburgh can proceed in order," and Mr. Smith proceeded with his argument, for he was now cool enough to argue the case. The rule against secret societies was adopted after a hard struggle, and went into the Discipline as law. It cost the connection thousands of members, and shut the Wesleyans out of many places where they might otherwise have collected good Churches.

The Conference adopted the "True Wesleyan" as its organ, and ordered it moved from Boston to New York, and provided for a Book Concern, and elected

Brother Scott Book Agent, and elected me editor of the "True Wesleyan" and also editor of the "Juvenile Wesleyan," a monthly Sunday-school paper, which it ordered published. I was also required to edit all Sunday-school books. So I had work enough laid out for me if much was to be done.

There were some other changes made in the Discipline, but nothing very essential. When the Conference adjourned Mrs. Lee and I started for home as we came. We reached a point in Ashtabula County, Ohio, on Saturday, where we spent a Sabbath on our way out and put up for the Lord's rest. When Monday morning came I changed my plan.

It was getting late in autumn, and I was anxious to get home, with a view of getting to my new post of labor and responsibility, where I was needed. As I was to remove from Syracuse to the City of New York, my horse and buggy had to be disposed of, and so I concluded to sell out there, and take a boat to Buffalo. We went to Fair Haven, to take a boat, but the wind was so high and the lake so rough that no boats came into that place. We could see them pass at a distance, but none dared to make that landing. After waiting until patience was exhausted in that direction, we took the stage, and that night we had the most terrible blow that ever visited the lakes. We were in the stage all night, and it was fearful; we were afraid the wind would blow the stage over. It was very dark, and was literally a

18

night of terror; and yet we thanked God that we were not on the lake, as we had tried hard to be. When the day began to dawn, as we approached the city of Erie, the effects of the storm became visible, and could be seen on both sides of the way. The presidential issue was pending between Polk and Clay, and the Democrats had erected hickory poles, and the Whigs had erected ash poles. All along the way the hickory had withstood the storm, but the ash poles were all blown down, usually broken near the ground, and lay prostrate. This was regarded by the Democrats as an omen of success, and the result accorded with their desires.

As we approached Buffalo more fearful effects of the storm were visible. Wrecked vessels were seen scattered along the shore, and in the city, bordering on the lake, the destruction was terrible. The storm drove down the lake, and so violent was it that it flooded portions of the city, and houses had been broken to pieces by the waves, and vessels were seen lying perfectly dry, many rods from the docks, up business streets. No vessels out had escaped undamaged, and many vessels and lives had been lost. We were thankful that we did not succeed in obtaining a passage on the lake, though we had a night of terror on the land.

From Buffalo we made a quick passage home, and every energy was exerted to get moved to our new field of labor and responsibility.

CHAPTER XXXIV.

The First Four Years of my Editorship—Difficulties in my
Way—Abundant Labors—Eulogy on Orange Scott.

THE editorship of our connectional paper involved
serious responsibilities and great difficulties. The
connection might be said to be a unit on the subject
of slavery; but it was greatly divided and heteroge-
neous in regard to other subjects, and it was doubtful
if it could be held together. We had many good
and true men who could be relied upon for any thing
reasonable, but we also had many restless, imprac-
ticable men, and some of them were strong men, and
others very weak men, and it was doubtful which
were the most dangerous to our unity and success.
The question of Church government was settled in
the "Discipline," but not in the minds of the people.
Some wanted a strong government and an absolute
appointing power to assign the preachers to their
fields of labor from year to year. Others were opposed to all control, and wished to be left free to
select their own fields of labor, as they could agree
with people. I leaned to the liberal side, but not
to the extreme. I understood perfectly well what
many did not appear to realize, namely, that neither
extreme could be adopted and carried out. I knew
we had not enough connectional adhesive power

to hold us together under a strong absolute appointing power; many ministers and many Churches would not submit to it. On the other hand, our ministers and people, as a whole, had not sufficient stability, union, and experience to manage, successfully, an extremely liberal system of Church polity, and the only hope was to run on a middle line between the two extremes; and that was no easy task for the helmsman with such rocks on both sides, with winds blowing both ways.

The secret-society question was of all others most exciting, and for a time cost me more trouble than any other; and but for the fact that neither side could count me among the *pros* or *cons*, I could not have held things together. I dared not let one side know what the other side said, or wished to say; and while the paper assumed to maintain free discussion, I published only rather temperate articles, while I burned up numbers of violent ones, not daring to let their contents be seen, and of the contents of which I have never told a friend to this day. In all such cases I wrote private appeals to the parties whose articles I did not publish, exerting all the skill and influence I had to calm them down and persuade them that it was best for the whole that their articles should not be published. It was a difficult matter, but I had been placed at the helm, and was determined to run our new ship clear of the rocks on both sides. Things gradually softened down; some of the more violent ones left, and others were modified, and the connection acquired more adhesive power as it grew older.

During my editorial career I had also to maintain a fight against common foes; for we were assailed on every side, and for some time we were made the target for all the political and ecclesiastical marksmen to shoot at, from popguns to the heaviest ordnance, and the "True Wesleyan," with its editor, was the center spot to aim at. Odds were against me, but I believed my cause to be just. I had large experience in controversy, and I defended myself and the connection as best I could, but with what skill I will not attempt to say; those who lived then, and were interested, must judge, if any such are still living. The battle of those times cannot be fully appreciated now, since the exciting waves of more than thirty-six years have swept the space which lies between this time and that. If my record of those first years of my editorial career could be placed before the public and read again, it would reveal two facts at least, namely, that I was not cowardly, and that I was not lazy.

I edited without any assistance two papers, the weekly "Wesleyan," and the semi-monthly "Juvenile Wesleyan," a Sunday-school paper. I preached or lectured nearly every Sabbath, and made frequent dashes off into the country, to lecture on slavery and temperance. I also took part in other leading dis-

cussions of those times, among which was that waked
up by the Adventists, who began to contend for the
seventh day as the Sabbath, and to deny the immortality of the soul. I wrote and published a "Treatise
on the Immortality of the Soul," which was a pioneer
work on the subject. Several works have since been
written on the subject. Those years, as I look back
to them, appear with the vividness, and almost like
the impressions left by a troubled dream. So much
had I to do, so intensely was my mind engaged, and
so much solicitude did I feel, that I took but little
note of the lapse of time. Nevertheless, time pursued its rapid course, and the first four years of my
editorial career were brought to a close in the fall
of 1848.

One great source of mental trouble was the failing
health of Brother Scott. He was the publishing
agent and sole financial manager of the Concern, and
it appeared to me it would be extremely difficult, if
not impossible, to run the newly-organized Concern
without him, and yet he was obviously failing, gradually wasting with consumption. He went lower
and lower, until he was confined to his room, when
his death became only a question of time with me,
though he seemed to cling to hope. The blow finally
fell; he died, and I felt it as one of the most severe
calamities of my life. I preached and published his
funeral sermon, from which I give the following
extract:

Orange Scott was an extraordinary man. During his sunny days in the Methodist Episcopal Church few were more popular, and none led on the embattled hosts of Methodism against their common foes with a bolder front, and to more certain victory, than did Orange Scott. Some had more scholastic polish, and some blew more silver-toned instruments; but his was the trump of God sounding the notes of uncompromising truth, and at the well-known sound more were rallied from the valleys and hills and rocky cliffs of New England than by the notes of any other trumpeter that ever yet passed that way. He died without a struggle; he departed as departs the sun when it goes down without a cloud, leaving a lingering glory upon the hills in evidence that it has not expired or lost its light, but is a sun still, traveling in its glory, though visible only to other spheres. He left us as leaves the morning star when it melts away and is lost amid the beams of the solar orb.

CHAPTER XXXV.

Second General Conference—Re-elected Editor with some opposition—Resigned in the Spring of 1852, and accepted the Pastorate of my old Church in Syracuse.

THE second General Conference was held in the city of New York, in the autumn of 1848. It was, on the whole, a quiet Conference. Daniel Worth was elected president, and L. C. Matlack was elected secretary. I was elected chairman of the Committee on Revisals.

I introduced some changes in regard to the appointing power, and the corresponding rights and powers of preachers and Churches. These amendments were not intended to change any thing fundamentally, but only to simplify and make the law and practices harmonize, which they did not. There had been also a difference of opinion in regard to the meaning of the rules in question, which I intended to obviate. My amendments were adopted by the Conference, but met with determined opposition during the next four years from Rev. Edward Smith and some others who followed his lead, and there arose a party who opposed the new edition of the rules. It was charged that a blow at the itinerancy had been struck. There was some warm discussion, and the matter was carried into the next General

Conference to be settled, as will be noticed in its chronological order.

There was one other matter which constituted an item in the Conference. In all such bodies, great or small, there will be persons who will seek for a place, though it be a small place. There were some members who believed they could edit the " True Wesleyan " more to their own satisfaction than I did, and there were as many as three of this class, if not more.

Just before the election of the editor was entered upon a resolution was introduced censuring the editor of the "Wesleyan" for the course he had pursued in regard to politics. I never had any politics which were not a part of my religion, and I had urged men to vote the Liberty ticket as a religious duty. My friends and my enemies, if I had any, I suppose, were astonished that I declined saying a word in self-defense. Finally Brother M'Gee, from Wisconsin, formerly of Northern New York, took the floor in defense of the editor, and the way he laid out these non-political Christians was workmanlike. I thought myself a good debater on politics in those days, but I was willing to yield him the palm. The resolution of censure was voted down.

When the election of editor came off I was elected on the first ballot. I thought that those who wanted the place did not know what it cost me in toil and mental anxiety, and I resolved I would never allow myself again to be a candidate, and told a friend so.

I labored on as I had done in time past, devoting all my energies to the interests of the paper and the Wesleyan cause. I responded to various calls from different localities to lecture on antislavery and temperance, and in defense of the Wesleyan organization.

In the spring of 1852 I resigned my position as editor to accept a pastorate. I was invited to take charge of the Church in Syracuse, which I had organized nine years before. As their Conference assembled in the spring, to step into their pastorate at the right time I had to vacate the editorial chair about five months before the close of my term, and the Rev. L. C. Matlack, who was publishing agent, took my place, and I hastened away to my new field of labor.

CHAPTER XXXVI.

In Syracuse—The Third General Conference—A Challenge
—A Debate on the Doctrine of the Trinity.

ON entering upon my pastoral labors among my
old friends in Syracuse I felt the great change.
Though I never made a pastoral charge a play-
ground, nor a resting-place to lounge and loll in the
shade, the transition from the solicitude and the
early and late office labors and nervous nights was so
great that for a few weeks I felt as though I was on
a vacation and must return to my toil.

The third Wesleyan General Conference assembled
in Syracuse in October, 1852. There was but little
transacted which constitutes a part of my biography,
except the discussion and action on the amended
rules, which I introduced as chairman of the Committee on Revisals, referred to in the preceding
chapter.

Two parties now existed, and the matter had been
discussed in the paper, and it was well understood
that the subject would come up for action in the
General Conference. The most important part I
acted in it was a newspaper feat just on the eve of
Conference, in reply to a very remarkable article.

Rev. Edward Smith had become an advocate of

an absolute appointing power, which appeared to exclude laymen from all right to any voice in the matter. I knew that to adopt and carry out his views would break up the Wesleyan Connection, for which I was not ready, and I opposed him. He undertook a stroke of policy by writing a long article entitled, "The Priesthood of Revealed Religion," which he intended should settle the question. This he sent to the "Wesleyan" on the eve of the General Conference, presuming no reply could be made through the paper until after Conference. The "Wesleyan" was published in the city of New York, and I was in Syracuse; of course, it was not supposed that I could receive the paper, then write a reply, and get it to New York soon enough to have it put in type in season to appear in the next paper.

The moment the editor received Smith's manuscript he wrote to me to secure my attention, and have me at home to attend to business. He put Smith's article on the page which was first set up, and sent me what printers call "galley slips" as fast as it was set up. The article filled nearly a page of the paper. The moment I got the first slip I commenced writing a reply, and as fast as a sheet was finished I sent it away, so that my reply was written by the time Smith's article was issued from the press. As fast as my sheets were received at the office they were given to the printer, and were all in type in season for the inside of the next issue, so that my reply, which filled a page, followed Smith's "Priesthood of Revealed Religion" in the next paper. Of the merits of the two papers I need not speak.

The two parties rallied in the Conference, and after skirmishing to save time, it was agreed that Smith should have a hearing, and that I should reply, and that the question should be put without further debate. A decided majority voted on the liberal side, and Brother Smith never made any more public fight on the subject.

A class of persons in those days were in the habit of holding union conventions in the interest of the overthrow of all denominational distinctions and all creeds. One of these conventions was held in Syracuse, and I went in to see and hear and learn what could be said against Church organizations and creeds.

The Rev. Samuel J. May, a distinguished Unitarian minister, and pastor of the Unitarian Church in Syracuse, was also present. Mr. May got into a discussion about creeds with a lay member of the Congregational Church, a particular friend of mine, and I put in a word which led to a slight pass between Mr. May and myself, and I thought nothing more of it. A week or ten days after I received a challenge from Mr. May to discuss the doctrine of the trinity with him. I accepted, and we debated eleven evenings in the City Hall, each speaking thirty minutes, and making two speeches of an evening on each side.

Mr. May was a remarkable man, not so much for his profound erudition, as for his gentlemanly bearing and benevolence. He was better known in the city than I was, but I offset his prestige by a frank, open, honest, and earnest manner.

The large hall was densely crowded every evening with the most learned and pious people in the city. So intense was the interest felt that the principal pastors of the city were at my house every day during the discussion, to inquire after my health, and to tender any help they could render in the hasty preparation of my rejoinders to his replies. My direct arguments I had carefully prepared in advance. The question was stated in the words of the first article of all Methodist creeds, as follows:

There is but one living and true God, everlasting, of infinite power, wisdom and goodness, the maker and preserver of all things, visible and invisible. And in unity of this Godhead there are three persons, of one substance, power, and eternity, the Father, the Son, [the Word,] and the Holy Ghost.

I had the affirmative, and must open the debate. After a brief introduction I stated my plan of argument as follows:

The first part of this article I understand is admitted by both parties to the discussion. The second part, commencing with the affirmation that "there are three persons in unity of the Godhead," is the real question in debate. Of this I have the affirmative, and my friend the negative. As I have the case to make out, I shall attempt to prove:

1. The essential, underived divinity of our Lord Jesus Christ—the Son or the Word.

2. The divinity of the Holy Ghost, and his personality.

3. The unity of the two with the Father, in the Godhead.

The course I pursued was to open each speech after the first with a brief rejoinder to his reply, and then prosecute the direct argument to the end of my half hour. By this course I kept my argument clear and distinct before the audience until it was finished, closing in, closer and closer, upon my opponent as I progressed. When I reached the end my summing up was brief, logical, and beyond the reach of an answer, as it was too late for my opponent to go back and attempt to refute my arguments upon which my conclusions rested. This he had failed to do as they were delivered, but had rather sought to amuse himself with his own objections to, and caricatures on, the doctrine of the Trinity, which I brushed from my path as I proceeded; and now I wound my chain of argument around him after this manner:

1. I have proved that the Son or Word is God, to him being applied all the names and titles of God, and he possessing all the attributes of God, performing all the works of God, and receiving the worship due only to God.

2. I have proved that the Holy Ghost is God, being known by the names and titles of God, possessing all the attributes of God, and being manifested in all the personal acts of God.

From these two points proved, it follows that they exist in union with the Father, making the doctrine of the Trinity true, or else that there are three Gods.

But there are not, and cannot be three Gods.

1. Both parties to this discussion affirm that "there is but one living and true God."

2. The Scriptures teach that there is but one God.

3. The conclusion that the Son and Holy Ghost, both being proved to be God, exist with the Father in the unity of the Godhead, is not only a necessary conclusion from the premises, but I have proved the doctrine of the Trinity by arguments which my opponent neither has answered nor can answer.

The arguments by which the points here affirmed were proved are not given, as a matter of course. Nor have I given my rejoinders to his replies, so far as he offered any. These would fill a volume. I will only add that the discussion resulted satisfactorily to all Trinitarians. My opponent, under the heavy pressure of my arguments, denied the pre-existence of Christ, denied his miraculous conception, and affirmed that he was the natural son of Joseph and Mary. When further pressed he denied the genuineness of the accounts of his conception and birth, and affirmed that they were forgeries, interpolated long after the Gospels were written. He had every appearance of honesty and candor in the opening of the discussion, and I believe he thought he had the right side of the question, and expected to be able to triumphantly defend his views and overthrow what he regarded as the absurdities of Trinitarianism. It appeared to me that he had been educated a Unitarian, and taught from his youth to believe that Trinitarianism was a concatenation of impossibilities, absurdities, and contradictions, which he had only to touch with his wand of reason to see the whole system fall to pieces. He appeared not to understand Trinitarianism, and to have no conception of the chain of iron-linked logic by which it could be defended. When he came to face an opponent quite as experienced in debate as himself, and who had thoroughly studied both sides of the question, he found the discussion any thing but the pleasant recreation he had anticipated, and was driven to positions he little thought of when he commenced the debate. He departed this life some years since, and I cannot tarry many years longer before I must cross over, when we may meet again, unless one of us shall have missed our way and fatally wandered from the path which leads to the destiny for which the Creator designed all me

19

CHAPTER XXXVII.

Invited to Fulton—Published my Book entitled, "Elements of Theology"—Elected Professor of Theology in Leoni College—Fourth General Conference—My Resignation of the Professorship.

AT the close of my three-years' labor in Syracuse I was invited to the pastorate of the Wesleyan Church in Fulton in the spring of 1855. This had been my last charge in the Methodist Episcopal Church, and now I returned as a Wesleyan pastor of a Wesleyan Church, after the absence of nearly seventeen years. Time had produced great changes both in myself and my old friends whom I left in the Methodist Episcopal Church. In my absence a Wesleyan Church had been organized, and a house of worship erected, and they appeared to be in a reasonably flourishing condition.

It was believed, both by myself and the Church, that my pastorate with them would be a long one, if not the closing one of my life; but, alas! how little we know what the future has in store for us! My pastorate lasted only one year, but was one of the most quiet and enjoyable years of my shifting and stormy life. During my three years in Syracuse, and the first half of my year in Fulton, I had written my work entitled "Elements of Theology," and had it ready for the press, but had no means to publish it. On the recommendation of Rev. L. C. Matlack, now Dr. Matlack, C. G. Case, Esq., a layman of my Church, advanced one thousand dollars to aid in publishing the work. I say on the recommendation of Brother Matlack, for I should never have asked for the money if my manuscript had lain unpublished to the close of my life.

As the close of my first year at Fulton was approaching I was surprised beyond measure by the visit of Rev. S. A. Baker, agent of the Leoni College, in Michigan, who said he was sent to engage my services as Professor of Theology. It surprised me, as they had never corresponded with me, and I had never thought of such a thing. I told him frankly I would not leave my people without their consent, and that I would not ask their consent, but that he might try and obtain their consent if he could. I did not believe he could, because I did not know his skill, and what persuasive and honeyed words he could utter. He urged the wants of the college, the advantage it would be to our young and rising denomination to have a theological department in the college, and what an advantage it would be to obtain my services, in view of the fact that I was the author of a system of theology which would be the text-book of the department. He finally promised to give me an acre of land, and put a good house upon it for a permanent home. The result was he obtained the following answer from Brother Case, who was our principal man, and spoke for the Church: "We have always wanted to get Brother Lee since we organized our Wesleyan Church, but he was otherwise engaged, and when we secured him we intended to keep him and take care of him, and those of us who should outlive him should bury him in our beautiful cemetery; but we will not stand in the way of an important general interest; if the wants of the school are as you state, you must take him."

Of course the matter was settled, and I was to remove to Michigan after the session of the Conference, at which time the Church could obtain a pastor to take my place. I filled out the programme, and arrived in Leoni about the first of May, 1856. Things did not look very promising, but I was enlisted and must fight the battle as best I could. I found a warm-hearted class of friends connected with the school, good and true, ready to do all that could be done with the means they could command, and even more; for some of them made great personal sacrifices to sustain the school. But still things looked unpromising to me, as though the undertaking was larger than resources would warrant. The acre of land was given and the house was erected, and we took possession. Public worship was maintained in the school building used as a church on the Sabbath, and I was appointed preacher. I could not very properly be called pastor, in view of my other engagement. A theological class was organized, and I took charge of it. It embraced some promising young men, some of whom are now successful preachers. I also taught a class in mental and moral science and another in history.

The fourth Wesleyan General Conference was held in Cleveland, Ohio, in October, 1856. I was elected president. Nothing occurred beyond regular business, and it proved a very quiet session.

As we approached the autumn of 1857 I became satisfied that the college was becoming hopelessly involved financially. I told the trustees my fears, but they saw things differently. I was getting personally involved, but could yet clear myself by a sufficient sacrifice ; but if I remained another year I should be hopelessly in debt. My salary was unpaid, and I could not see how it was to be paid, and it never was paid. I sold my furniture to pay some debts I had contracted, and sold my house for as much as I had put in it from my own resources, leaving it so that by paying that amount the college could recover it. This gave me funds enough to remove me to some other field of labor, and I resigned and went to a new scene of labor and responsibility.

CHAPTER XXXVIII.

Remove to Felicity, Ohio—A Two Years' Pastorate—Remove to Chagrin Falls — Oration on John Brown — Fifth General Conference—Appointed Connectional Missionary —Very Sick and Resign—Another Pastorate—Elected Professor—Remove to Adrian, Mich.—Sixth and last General Conference.

HAVING resigned my professorship at Leoni, I accepted of the pastorate of a Wesleyan Church at Felicity, Clermont County, Ohio. I commenced my labors in September, 1857, and served the Church two years. It was while I was in this pastorate that I was struck with the title of Doctor of Divinity. It came from Middlebury College, Vermont. All I can say about it is, that it came as a surprise to me, as I had no previous knowledge of any such intention, and had never asked for or had any expectation of any such honor, and did not know that any of my friends thought of or asked for any such favor on my behalf.

There was nothing remarkable occurred during this pastorate except a little under-ground railroad work, which may be noted in a special chapter on that subject. I closed my two years' labor in Felicity, September, 1859, and removed to Chagrin Falls, Ohio. I preached here to a Wesleyan and Congregational

Church, who united in my support, and worshiped in one congregation.

While here I preached and published a funeral sermon for John Brown, whom brave old Virginia, who never tires, succeeded in hanging. He was buried in North Elba, in north-eastern New York, by the side of a rock under the shadow of the Adirondack Mountains. Wendell Phillips delivered an oration over his grave when he was buried. He had a little home in this wild region on a piece of land which had been given him by Gerrit Smith. On the 4th of July, 1860, I was called from my home in Ohio to deliver an oration from the rock overhanging John Brown's grave. That was the oration of my life, the most radical and, probably, the most able I ever delivered. I loaned the manuscript to a reporter present, who promised to return it, but I have never seen it since.

The Brown family were all present, but I have not seen one of them since. As I came down from the rock at the close of the oration I shook hands with each of the family, and as I took the hand of the second son he said : " It electrifies my arm clear up to my shoulder and makes my heart jump to take hold of your hand."

While at Chagrin Falls I was called to Adrian, Michigan, to deliver the oration at the laying of the corner-stone of the principal college building.

The fifth General Conference assembled at Fulton,

N. Y., in October, 1860, of which I was a member. Rev. L. C. Matlack was elected president. This was a quiet Conference, and but little transpired which can properly fill space in my personal history. One little tilt may be named. I had a slight passage at arms with some extremist on the subject of dress. My position was, that we could not frame specific rules which should determine just what persons should wear and should not wear. I insisted that the best results would be secured by enforcing plainness of dress on scriptural authority ; that legislating concerning the cut of coats and the number of buttons to be put upon them, or the size and shape of bonnets, and the length and breadth of ribbon with which they should be trimmed, could do no good. I said it must be allowable to wear gold in some cases. The Church required a minister to put a gold ring on the finger of a bride, and I could not see how it could be right for me to put gold on a lady's finger which it would be wrong for her to wear. I said I had never worn gold in any form, because I was too poor, but if some friend should present me with golden-bowed spectacles I should wear them without committing sin. The next day I was invited to call on a friend, when I found a small party of friends in his parlor, one of whom, with an appropriate address, presented me with a pair of gold-bowed spectacles. This was twenty-one years ago, and those gold bows are worn out and I am using cheaper ones.

At this General Conference I was elected a general missionary to travel through the whole connection to preach, lecture, organize Churches, and promote its interests. I removed from Ohio, and located my family in Syracuse, N. Y., and entered upon my work with more zeal and energy than was prudent in the circumstances. It proved to be a very severe winter, and, in addition to other exposures, I lay out in the cars, under snow blockades, on different routes, five nights in all. I took one cold after another; still I kept on laboring, until I was compelled to desist, and returned home very sick on the first of March. Many of my friends thought I was near my end, but, by the blessing of God, I recovered. About the last of April I began to mend, and improved very rapid-ly. But I gave up all hope of being able to prosecute my mission, and resigned.

The Syracuse Conference met the last of April, and I accepted of the pastorate of a very light charge at Sprague's Corners, on the line between Jefferson and St. Lawrence Counties. The country was under great excitement with the opening scenes of the great Rebellion. This section of the country was very pa-triotic, and, it having been my old stumping-ground in my palmy days in the Methodist Episcopal Church, I was well known, and was called out for speeches at pole raisings and public meetings for raising troops for the war, and did what I could.

I remained in this pastorate, in comparative seclusion, three years, and was resolved never again to appear so prominently before the public as I had done for the past thirty years of my active and stormy life. I was now in my sixtieth year, and took measures to secure me a permanent home, with a view of spending and closing a peaceful end of life in this quiet and out-of-the-way place; but my plan was overruled, and I was pushed out from my moorings, and I found myself again at sea.

In the latter part of the winter of 1864 I received a letter from the Rev. Cyrus Prindle, and another from C. G. Case, of Fulton, urging me not to engage to serve my Church any longer than to the Conference in the spring, as a plan was put in motion to secure for me a theological professorship in Adrian College. Adrian College was a new Wesleyan institution of learning at Adrian, Mich. In due time I received official notice of my election. I accepted, and removed to Adrian in the spring of 1864. In the discharge of my new duties I organized a class in theology, of which I had exclusive charge, and taught the branches of theology and homiletics. I also organized a class in natural theology. And to relieve the other professors, who were overtaxed, I took a class in both mental and moral science.

In the autumn of 1864 the sixth Wesleyan General Conference was held in Adrian. This was the last I attended. I was again elected president, which placed me in the chair three times out of six.

CHAPTER XXXIX.

Financial Embarrassment of the College—Proposed Union with the Protestant Methodists—Its Failure—The College changes hands—I Resign and Return to the Methodist Episcopal Church.

THE war and its results, with the change of the Methodist Episcopal Church from a pro-slavery to an antislavery position, removed the principal reason for the Wesleyan Methodist organization. The Wesleyans lost their influence and progressive power, as other denominations became more and more antislavery, and from the commencement of the war they began to decline. The college was financially involved, and great efforts were made to relieve it without success. A proposition was made to unite with the Protestant Methodists as a mode of relief, and also as a measure of Christian union upon principle. This measure I did not favor in its early stages, not that I was opposed to such a union, but because my knowledge of the elements we had to deal with led me to believe such a union impossible, and I wanted no fuss and failure. Others pressed it until I saw there would be trouble, and then I went in for the union as a last hope, and pushed it with all the power and influence I had, believing success alone could save us from utter ruin.

In anticipation of the consummation of the union the Protestants were let into college in half interest under provisions which promised legal consolidation, when the ecclesiastical union should be completed. The Protestants had a fund which they had raised for the purpose of founding a college, which they now held in reserve until the question of union should be settled.

There now arose a terrible outcry by Wesleyans opposed to union, urging the fact that there were Masons in the Protestant Methodist Church, this making the proposed union as wicked as a union with hell.

In a public convention they denounced the proposed union, and condemned the Board of Trustees for selling out the rights of the Wesleyans in the college to the Protestants. There was no truth in this; we had sold nothing; the college was on the verge of financial ruin, and must be lost, and we were trying to save one half of it at least. I was President of the Board of Trustees, and I did not bear the charge very meekly, as much as I had labored for the Wesleyans, for as poor pay as I had received, from men who had never given a dollar to the college and would not lift a finger to save it. I replied with deserved severity. I would have been glad to have retired from the whole concern, if those who were opposed to union would have taken the college upon their hands; but they would not, and could not have done it if they

would; it was upon us, and we determined to con-
summate the union, and take as many with us as would
go, which, of course, would carry the college into the
union.

Just at this point a plot was developed by a selfish
Protestant connected with the college to secure control, and make himself president by slander and falsehood directed against some of my friends. This plot
was not directed at me, for I was not president,
nor did I expect or wish to be; but it was so false,
corrupt, and vile, that I could not consent to co-
operate with any person who would be guilty of such
an act, and yet I had no redress but to back square
out of the union, and this was the step I determined
to take.

In consultation with friends, whom I knew I could
trust, I told them I was going to the Methodist Episcopal Church, and if they would go with me we
would make an effort to save the college by carrying
it with us. The largest number consented. The
Rev. John M'Eldowney, who was President of the
Faculty, and myself, who was President of the Board
of Trustees, called upon the Rev. F. A. Blades, who
was presiding elder of the district, and laid the whole
case and our plan before him. He received our
proposition favorably, and promised to co-operate
with us to the extent of his ability. We then went
openly and earnestly to work. One half of the
trustees were Wesleyans, all of whom were in sympa-

thy with our proposition. The other half of the trustees were citizens, and not Wesleyans. An exciting contest now arose between us Wesleyans and the Protestants. At first the citizen trustees rather stood aloof from taking a decisive part in the struggle, but when they saw that the Protestants had the money in hand, and offered to pay the debts of the college, if it were given over to them, they took sides with them. Still we held them at bay for a time, but as some of our trustees resided at a distance, even out of the State, it was difficult, and as we had not the means of securing the debts, and as the Protestants had the cash in hand, we could not hold out long, and finally resigned, and the college passed into the hands of the Protestants.

Notwithstanding I had been most active in the struggle and been their principal opposer, they wished to retain me in my professorship, and sent the Hon. L. G. Berry to me, as a committee from them, to inquire if they could effect a reconciliation with me and retain me in the college. I frankly told him it was impossible for me to consent to remain with them. I might have retained my position in the college, and might, probably, have been comfortably seated in a professor's chair to-day, if I could have consented to act in harmony with those whom I believed to be false and dishonest.

It was not the first time I had been compelled to turn away from what appeared to be for my worldly advantage to preserve my integrity, but it was doubt-less the last time I shall be called upon to make such a sacrifice, as I am now too far advanced in life to be worth buying.

It was early in the spring of 1867 when I with others resigned and left the college, and the Detroit Methodist Episcopal Annual Conference was not to hold its session until September. I might have been received at once by a Quarterly Conference, but my friend, Bishop Kingsley, said that course would be less direct, and might embarrass my reception into the Annual Conference, and advised me to wait until the meeting of that body, and bring the question before them, as that would render the case clear and simple. From that day I was regarded and treated as a minister of the Methodist Episcopal Church. I was immediately employed as a supply for the Rev. W. H. Shine, of Port Huron, for eight Sabbaths, while he recreated his impaired health.

I was then employed by the presiding elder to supply the Franklin Charge, whose preacher's health had failed, and he soon died. I labored on this charge until the meeting of the Conference, when I and others were received as ministers coming from the Wesleyan Methodist Connection. I suppose, however, there must have been an exception in my case. As I was one of the organizers of the Wesleyan Methodist Connection, and was in Methodist Episcopal orders at the time, I had no Wesleyan papers to present. I therefore sent in my parchments, signed by Bishop Roberts and Bishop Soule, and my certificate of location, signed by Bishop Morris, dated 1838, showing that twenty-nine years had made their flight since I located. I suppose the paper was not regarded as outlawed, as I was received, and all my papers returned to me, and not a word was said.

CHAPTER XL.

My Reception into the Detroit Conference—My Return to the Methodist Episcopal Church Defended.

I WAS received into the Detroit Annual Conference of the Methodist Episcopal Church, at its session at Saginaw City, in September, 1867. There were six of us admitted at the same time. Our names being called, we advanced to the altar, when the Bishop asks the question, "Will you conform to the Discipline and usages of the Methodist Episcopal Church?" This question being answered in the affirmative, Rev. Mr. Blades, presiding elder of the Adrian District, introduced us to Conference, using in substance the following language:

These are Wesleyan brethren, who have been ministers in the Wesleyan Connection, who are now to be received into the ministry of the Methodist Episcopal Church. It gives me great pleasure to introduce them to the Conference, and especially does it give me pleasure to refer to one of them by name.

Dr. Lee, who stands before you for admission to the Conference, comes to us for re-admission. He entered the ministry of the Methodist Episcopal Church in early life, in which he spent some of the best days of his manhood. His zeal, energy, and success were known among the Churches, and gave him a name which has not been forgotten. But there arose a great question, on which he judged it his duty to leave the Church, believing that by so doing, he could more effectually oppose the monster evil which was subordinating Church and

20

State. He left honestly. He has fought the battle bravely, ever being found in the thickest of the fight. He has fought until he has heard the shout of victory, and now that the battle is over, he returns to seek a home in the Church of his early choice.

To be sure, he returns not as he left, in the full vigor of early manhood, but he comes bearing the impress of years, and with whitened locks, which have been bleached upon the moral battle-fields which he has so nobly contested; but he is yet strong and brave, and ready for service, and it gives me great pleasure to introduce him and his brethren, who stand here with him: and in the name of the Conference I bid them welcome. I hope Dr. Lee will speak a few words for himself and in behalf of his brethren.

I made a few remarks under the influence of very great emotion, in which the whole congregation appeared to participate, for there were but few if any eyes in the house which did not weep. I closed my remarks by turning to the Bishop and offering my hand, saying: "Will you take my hand, in behalf of these my brethren?"

The Bishop rose and, taking my hand, he said: "Yes, I will take your hand and theirs too," and proceeded to give each of them the right hand of fellowship.

As the shaking of hands was finished, the whole assembly rose to their feet and sang, "Praise God, from whom all blessings flow."

My return to the Methodist Episcopal Church was condemned by old Wesleyan friends, who refused to go with me, and persisted in maintaining the Wesleyan organization. They said hard things, and declared that I had stultified myself, and proved recreant to my principles. I do not know that any defense against these charges is necessary; yet, as I have frankly given my reasons for leaving the Church, it is proper and consistent that I should give my reasons for returning to the Church I left. I assign a general reason which comprehends the whole, when I say that I returned because the reason for which I left had ceased to exist. But I will be a little more specific.

1. I left the Methodist Episcopal Church solely on account of slavery, and but for slavery I should never have thought of leaving her; nor did I go back, nor talk nor think of going back, until she was entirely free from slavery.

2. When I left the Methodist Episcopal Church and assisted in organizing the Wesleyan Connection, I did not do it because I believed there were not Churches enough in number, but because I believed it was necessary to have one Church with which I could sympathize, and to which I could belong and co-operate with a good conscience. This was doing the only thing I could do in the circumstances, for I never thought of living without a Church, and when I found slavery in the Methodist Episcopal Church, and could not get it out, the only thing I could do was to organize a Church without slavery, which I did. And in these circumstances it was consistent for me to do what I did. I supported the Wesleyan

organization with all my powers, and I opposed the pro-slavery position and action of the Methodist Episcopal Church with equal zeal and power, and no one man did more, and made better fight than I did.

3. When slavery ceased to exist in the Methodist Episcopal Church, the reason for the two separate organizations ceased to exist, and it was proper that they should be united, and it was most proper that the smaller body should go to the larger, and so I led the way back to the Methodist Episcopal Church. That the whole body did not go with me was not my fault.

4. The Methodist Episcopal Church made such generous advances and such honorable concessions in regard to our course as antislavery Methodists and as opposed to their former course, as removed every objection, and enabled me to return without compromitting my principles, my honor, my consistency, or wounding my very sensitive nature. I walked back into the Methodist Episcopal Church as a long-absent son would walk into his reconciled mother's parlor, with whom he had differed in his youth, and separated himself.

A few facts only need be given to justify the above statement. The rules of the Church speak for themselves, and show that the Church has become organically antislavery in her constitutional law. But there has been other action. The General Conference has not only rescinded its own pro-slavery action of 1836 and 1840, but taken a positive stand against slavery by adopting the following resolutions:

Resolved, That we regard our national calamities as resulting from our forgetfulness of God and slavery, so long our nation's reproach, and that it becomes us to humble ourselves and forsake our sins as a people, and hereafter in all our laws and acts to honor God.

Resolved, That we are decidedly in favor of such an amendment to the Constitution, and such legislation on the part of the States, as shall prohibit slavery or involuntary servitude, except for crime, throughout all the States and Territories of the country.—*Gen. Conf. Jour.*, p. 264, 1864.

The official organs of the Church spoke in no uncertain language. The following items are sufficient:

The Wesleyan body has existed to a noble purpose. It has borne its unwavering testimony against slavery, and we have felt its influence to be salutary upon our more temporizing tone. The world will be grateful to them for the work they have done, and the old Church has, in every possible form, shown her present oneness of spirit with this noble body of Christians. . . . We turn with pleasure to the thought of a union between ourselves and these our Wesleyan brethren. Should they come among us they will find themselves in congenial associations.—*Western Advocate.*

We would that, in accordance with the resolution of our Bishops, our centennial year could be marked by a reunion of the different fragments of our American Methodism. Especially would we rejoice in the return of that Church—the Wesleyans—who seceded from us rather than make concessions to the Southern slave power. We honor and love those men. Their secession, as we believe, saved our Church in 1844 from accepting a slave-holding Bishop. They, honorably to themselves, left the Church for the Church's good. And for that same Church's good, we trust that they will return with a full, triumphant welcome.—*Methodist Quarterly Review.*

I will close this chapter with two brief remarks.

1. The taunt which impracticables have often hurled at me, that the Methodist Episcopal Church did not free itself from slavery until it was abolished in the State, is without force, though there is some truth in it. The Church struggled manfully to free itself from slave-holding by a change of her organic law, which required time, so that it was not accomplished until about the time of emancipation. While this is true, it is also true that the Methodist Episcopal Church contributed more influence and moral power to secure emancipation than any other one Church or class of people.

2. The decided and open and frank manner in which she has confessed her former wrong, and set herself right, proves her honesty and integrity in the matter. I am proud to belong to a Church which has had courage and moral strength enough thus to confess her wrong and set herself right.

CHAPTER XLI.

Fourteen Years in the Methodist Episcopal Church since my Return.

I WAS appointed to Court-street Church on my reception into the Detroit Conference, where I spent two pleasant and prosperous years. I was then appointed to Ypsilanti, where I remained but one year. It was a heavy charge, and in the latter part of the winter I took a severe cold while attending a funeral, and was quite sick, but was out of the pulpit but one Sabbath; yet I did not recover my usual health, and at the close of the year a change was desired, and I was sent to Northville. Here I labored in poor health, and at the end of the year I was placed upon the superannuated list. This was the severest trial of my life; but as my health was poor, and I was in my seventy-first year, nothing else could be expected. The Conference, by resolution, requested me to preach a semi-centennial sermon at its next session, which I did at East Saginaw, where the Conference was held in 1872.

In this sermon I remarked upon my antislavery efforts, and stated that I had been mobbed five times for opposing slavery, and that though I was never seriously injured, I had one new suit of clothes destroyed, for which the miscreants never paid me. The moment I closed my sermon Brother Arnold, now Dr. Arnold, sprang upon his feet, and said, "I move we pay Dr. Lee for that suit of clothes;" and it was no sooner said than done, and fifty dollars were contributed for my benefit.

Soon after this Conference the Milford Charge became vacant, and at the request of both the people and presiding elder I undertook to supply the work. On the last of November I was taken sick of typhoid fever, and run very low, and it was thought my departure was at hand. I listened for the sound of the coming boatman's oar, but it pleased God that I should recover. My health so improved that at the Conference for 1874 I was again placed upon the effective list, and appointed to Petersburgh, and filled the appointment for the year, though I did not move my family to the charge. I found good and kind-hearted brethren and sisters in Petersburgh, but as a charge they had been so reduced by deaths and removals, and other causes, that they were not able to give me such a support as would warrant me in removing my family from their comfortable home in Northville, and I secured a home for myself, and devoted myself to the work assigned me.

The fiftieth anniversary of our wedding occurred on the 31st of July, and was duly celebrated by the kindness of the brethren at our home in Northville. This anniversary, taken in all of its bearings, was one of the brightest spots in my life. I was poor and embarrassed, and without adequate means of meeting the real necessities of life. I had come among the brethren a stranger, old and gray-headed, only eight years before, three of which I had been superannuated, and felt that I had but a very slight claim upon their generosity. They, however, displayed a great interest, and made it a complete success, and crowned the occasion with a donation of more than four hundred and fifty dollars. The occasion, too, was a very enjoyable one. The Rev. Dr. Jacokes was president of the day, and after calling the company to order from their real social intercourse, a prayer was offered by Dr. Pilcher, after which the chairman made a very appropriate and beautiful presentation address.

Of course it was incumbent upon me to respond, which I did by reading the following poem :

> Welcome, kind friends, twice welcome here,
> We greet you all with hearty cheer,
>   On this our nuptial day ;
> Long years have sped since we were wed,
> Bright hopes have fled, and white our head
>   Has grown along our way.

> We then were young, but young grows old,
> So soon the tale of years is told,
>   And life's short journey run ;
> Life then was bright, our path was light,
> In manhood's might began the fight
>   Which now is almost won.

As for myself, you see my plight,
Time passed and left on me its blight,
   And rudely blew the blast;
With battered prow and furrowed brow,
A withered bough you see me now,
   A shadow of the past.

Behold my spouse, my bride once fair,
With deep blue eye and auburn hair,
   So comely in her prime;
Faded you see, yet fair is she,
And fair will ever be to me,
   Both in my eye and rhyme.

No man could have more faithful wife
To bless his home and cheer his life,
   And smooth his rugged way;
Ready to bear her equal share
Of toil and care, with patience rare—
   Such is the bride to-day.

Full fifty years, as groom and bride,
Have we two traveled side by side,
   Where'er our journey lay;
Through sun and shade, forest and glade,
Our mutual aid, our hearts have stayed,
   Through all the rugged way.

Remembered joys, remembered sorrow,
From departed years we borrow,
   All that is left of yore;
Joys have fled, hearts have bled,
Friends are dead, since we were wed,
   And life seems life no more.

The lingering charms of earth are few,
As from our present stand we view
   Life past so soon away;
The withered flower, the vanished hour,
The falling tower, the waving power,
   The mildew of decay.

Those years did fullest joy afford,
When children smiled around our board,
  Five sons, two daughters fair;
But years have sped, those joys have fled,
Our hearts have bled, three sons are dead,
  The living scattered—where?

Soft echoes from those happy years,
Still breathe sweet music in our ears,
  Like chimes from far-off dome;
But cannot cheer life's autumn drear,
Like voices clear we used to hear,
  When children caroled in our home.

That music is an empty dream,
Those echoes are not what they seem,
  This memory at its play
No prattles here our home to cheer,
But lone and drear we two appear,
  Still pressing on our way.

Careworn and weary here we stand,
United still in heart and hand,
  Despite the rugged past;
Naught can sever us forever,
Part we never, long, forever,
  Our golden ties shall last.

Our steps grow short, and well we know
That soon our union here below
  In death will find its close;
But faith grows bright, and with delight
We'll end the fight, and take our flight
  To realms of long repose.

The joys of earth soon pass away,
Its wealth and honor all decay—
  They perish in an hour;
Time takes its flight, but leaves its blight,
Subdues all might, and conquers quite
  All terrestrial power.

All unions here must have an end,
We all must lose or leave our friend,
    But friends shall meet again;
Where life shall thrill, death never chill,
Where joy shall fill, our union still
        For evermore. Amen.

Our golden wedding tells a tale—
We celebrate low in the vale,
    Down on the misty shore;
Where the river, flowing ever,
Two worlds sever, whence forever
        Those who cross return no more.

Our golden wedding! Since we wed,
Long fifty married years have sped,
    And brought the day and guest;
The brightest day, in all the way,
So blithe and gay, with golden ray,
        The day of all the rest.

Kind friends, we thank you for this call,
Deep in our hearts we thank you all,
    But words cannot reveal,
Nor tongue can tell, though long it dwell,
And heart shall swell, and tears shall well,
        The gratitude we feel.

And absent friends have sent their store
To swell your gifts and make them more;
    To them our thanks are due;
O were they here our hearts to cheer,
That they might hear our thanks sincere
        Expressed to them and you!

With thanks which words can never tell
Our hearts henceforth will ever swell
    And throb while life remains;
Immortal fire, intense desire,
Shall string our lyre, which ne'er will tire
        Of fervent grateful strains

We all may meet on earth no more,
But hope to meet on yonder shore,
　　Beyond the tide of time;
Where homes secure ever endure,
With water sure, from fountains pure,
　　In that immortal clime.

We linger on the strand awhile,
Waiting the Master's coming smile,
　　To light our passage o'er;
We'll drop the cross, we'll leave the dross,
Nor count it loss, the river cross,
　　To that eternal shore.

There will we join the wedding throng,
With angels sing the nuptial song,
　　The song that dries all tears;
Immortal choir, with hearts on fire,
With tongue and lyre, will never tire,
　　Through the eternal years.

Let us our garments all prepare,
That we may be admitted there,
　　Before the great I AM;
Nor be too late to celebrate,
Within the gate, in royal state,
　　The marriage of the Lamb.

At the close of this year I was returned to the superannuated list, not, I believe, because I had failed in my labors, for I preached twice every Sabbath, and was absent from my charge but two Sabbaths during the year. Of this no complaint was or could be made, as it was to pay a last visit to a dying son in Syracuse, N. Y., who departed this life July 20, 1875. He was our eldest son, and his death was severely felt by us all.

I have now been without an appointment for six years, and so firm has been my health that there has not been a Sabbath during these years upon which I might not have preached twice, and sometimes three times, on a Sabbath-day when there was a call for my labors. So firm did my health appear that at the Conference for 1878 I asked for an effective relation and to be given regular work again, which the Conference refused to grant for reasons better known to the individual voters than to myself and to many others. As in duty bound, I submitted to the will of the majority, I trust with Christian meekness, though I was then, and am now, satisfied that several charges which I should have been willing to have taken have not been any better served than they would have been under my ministry, old as I am.

The Conference, while it declined to give me regular work, adopted the following resolution, I believe unanimously :

Resolved, That having a high appreciation of the ripe experience and rare abilities of Rev. Luther Lee, D.D., both as a preacher and lecturer, and rejoicing that he yet retains so much vigor for such public efforts, notwithstanding his advanced age, we cheerfully commend him to the public, and will, where we find it practicable to do so, invite him to our pulpits, and ask our people to contribute to his support.

JOHN RUSSEL,
E. E. CASTER.

Since the above-described conference action in my case I have been trying to make the best of my opportunities, and have preached and lectured where I have been invited. As might have been expected, however, the condition in the resolution appears to have been its most potent clause : " Will, where we find it practicable to do so, invite him," has brought me but few invitations. A few have responded nobly, but many never found it "practicable." Being still able to preach or lecture twice on the Sabbath, and having now entered upon my eighty-first year, it must be admitted that I enjoy a green old age. To God be all the glory! Amen.

CHAPTER XLII.

Work on the Under-ground Railroad

MY life would appear imperfect indeed if nothing should be said about my connection with that wonderful institution, the "Under-ground Railroad." From about 1840 to the commencement of the War of the Rebellion the road did a large business, but I will not swell my pages with the many cases of which the public had authentic accounts as they occurred, but only relate a few cases in which I acted some part. The morality of assisting fugitive slaves was called in question by many in these early times; but I never had any scruples on the subject, nor had I much difficulty in defending myself on moral ground.

My ground was that slavery was wrong, and hence all laws which aided and supported it must be wrong. Any law which requires a citizen to do a morally wrong act, or to omit the performance of a moral duty, has no binding force, and every citizen is bound to disobey all such laws, and take the consequences rather than to disobey God.

I used also to urge the law of nature which is developed in every man. No man does or can believe it right that another should make a slave of him, and hence no slave does or can be made to believe that he is rightfully held as a slave. From this it must follow that all slaves believe they have a right to escape from their bondage when they can do so, and their moral right to do so no man can deny. If, then, a slave has a moral right to escape from his master, I must have a right to help him escape. What he has a right to do for himself I have a right to help him to do if he needs my help and I am in a condition to render such help. These arguments always satisfied myself, and never failed to silence opposers, if they did not convince them.

The first contested case in which I became personally interested was in the city of New York. A young man was arrested as a fugitive slave, and by some means escaped from the officer—I knew not how—and, being closely pursued, took shelter in a business house, and was concealed in the loft. At this point in the proceedings I became acquainted with the case. It was strongly suspected that the place was watched. After a time a cart was ordered to take a box of goods to a steamboat dock on the North River to be transported to Albany. This was at dusk of evening. As the box was about to be delivered it was seized by an officer, who removed the cover, and there was found a young colored man. Of course, he was held as the fugitive and locked up until the court should convene next morning. Meanwhile the blatant Abolitionists made loud demonstrations, which had no effect more than to suggest to the

21

officers to be watchful and make sure the safe keeping of their man. The next day, when the supposed fugitive was produced in court, it was seen at a glance that he was not the man who had been arrested and made his escape. The wrong man had been boxed up, and the real fugitive had improved a whole night and part of a day in placing a wide space between himself and those who were guarding his substitute in New York. He was safe.

Another case occurred which excited much interest and involved some of the mysteries of the Underground Railroad. A vessel from Brazil came into port with two slaves on board used as sailors. A writ of *habeas corpus* was issued on application of some of the meddlesome Abolitionists, and they were brought up for a hearing. The captain returned that they were his seamen, and that he held them as his seamen under a treaty between the United States and Brazil. The lawyer who was usually employed to attend to such cases was out of the city, and a young limb of the law was employed, who in reply to the return put in a demurrer which was fatal. I could have made a better reply myself, but I knew nothing about the case until after the decision on the pleading. The demurrer rested the case on the facts set forth in the return, which were sufficient in the absence of other facts, and it was now too late to affirm or prove any other facts, and the men were returned to the captain as his seamen. The attorney instead of demurring should have traversed and affirmed that while the men were used as seamen they were held as slaves contrary to the laws of the United States and of the State of New York. Another writ was obtained from another judge, to which the captain returned through his counsel by putting in a plea of *res judicata*, which affirms "the case has been judged," and the judge would not go behind the for-mer decision. A third writ was obtained from an-other judge, and served the moment the last decision was rendered. It was returnable on Monday at nine o'clock A.M. The captain turned to the keeper of the Eldridge-street jail and said, "It will not pay for me to take these men on board of my vessel to bring them back on Monday; take them and lock them up, and I will pay you for their board." "All right," said the jailer, and led them away. I was in the court room, a silent spectator, watching the case and hearing the battle between the lawyers. When I had heard the contract between the captain and the jailer I walked out and found a man I happened to know, who had more brains than tongue and more cunning than logic, and said to him, "Those men are not in the custody of the law, and will not be until nine o'clock on Monday. They are private boarders at the jail, and if they can be got out between this time and Monday it will not be jail-breaking."

It so happened that on Monday morning the men were gone, and no one knew how they got away. I was in the court on Monday when the court opened, to see and hear what might be said and done. The captain appeared with his attorney and made a return to the writ. It affirmed that the men described in the writ were in his custody on Saturday, that he left them in care of the keeper of the Eldridge-street jail, that when he called for them they were not there, and he did not know how they escaped nor whence they had gone. As no one doubted the truth of his return it relieved him of all responsibility, but his men were gone.

His attorney thought he must appear to earn his fee, and so blustered and raved a little, and declared that there had been treachery, that no man but a lawyer could have known that the men were not in the custody of the law. I said nothing, but I felt very sure there was one man who knew so much who had not the reputation of being a lawyer. The remarks were aimed at the opposite counsel, and intended to make the impression that he had dishonorably played sharp. This waked him up, and he filed an affidavit that no one had asked counsel of him and that he had given counsel to no person in regard to the men since the last decision by the court.

The jailer was sent for, and he made oath that the men were in the jail on Sunday night, and that on Monday morning they were gone; that he found the keys in their usual place, and no doors or windows were open or broken, and that there were no marks of violence, and that he had no knowledge of the manner in which they escaped. The judge, who was an aged, able, and very venerable man, put on a solemn face and said, "The only conclusion to which the court can come is that the men went out at the key-hole."

The facts were as follows: somebody—I never knew who—went in and had a good time with the jailer until a very late hour, and the result was the jailer slept very sound after he was gone. This same person who spent the evening with the jailer put a flea in the ear of a person who was locked up for a day or two for some small offense, and the flea in his ear caused him to wake up at twelve o'clock at night and go and get the keys and open the door and put the two men out, and then lock the door and put the keys in their place and go to his bunk. When the jailer got up in the morning he was doing a loud business in the line of snoring. Outside there was a carriage waiting for the men when they came out, into which they entered and were driven across the State line into Connecticut, and sent to Boston. A ship was on the point of sailing for Hayti, and they were put on board and sent to that island.

One of the two was a man advanced in life, and the other was a young man and had lately been stolen from Africa. He was a son of one of their petty kings, and was educated in Arabic, and I received a letter from him requesting me to send him an Arabic Bible, which I did. A few years after he returned to New York to improve his English education, and on learning that I had removed to Syracuse he came out and made me a visit, so grateful did he feel for the part I had acted in his behalf.

I will describe one more case which occurred in the city of New York. A young colored man was stopping in the city, and arose one Sunday morning at the dawn of day, and stepped out upon the sidewalk; he was knocked down, handcuffed, and thrown into a carriage and carried off before any alarm could be given. After making some search in vain his friends came to me for advice. All they knew was just what is stated above, and that, though it was a severe blow, was but a slight clew, as it left no trail. I would see what could be done. One of the supreme judges of the State residing in the city was my friend, and had invited me to call on him for counsel in such cases whenever I needed it, which he would give freely. I went to him and stated the case, and he told me nothing could be done until the man was found. If they had carried him South, that was the end of the matter; but if they had not carried him off yet we must find him. But how can that be done? was my question. He told me he knew one of the best detectives in the State, who would find him if above ground; "but," said he, "it will cost something, for he is a poor man and cannot work without pay." I told him I would go and consult with some interested parties and return and report what could be done. I soon returned and told him to start his detective, that I had good backers for his pay.

Now comes the process. The detective first examined all the principal lines of travel south, and satisfied himself that the man had not been removed far. He then made closer search about the city. He learned that he crossed the Brooklyn ferry. He must then be in Brooklyn or on Long Island. He then discovered a Baltimore clipper lying at anchor in the bay. In the character of a sailor he boarded her, and satisfied himself that there was no slave on board, but learned that she came in ballast, and in a few days was going back in ballast. This furnished material for thought. He said to himself, "That vessel did not come for nothing. If she came to take that slave back why did they not take him on board and sail at once? There can only be one answer, which is, There are others they wish to catch before they go back, and if this be true they have concealed that man on the island until the others are caught." Then he commenced his search, and found the man back on the island, chained in an old log-house, in a lonely place.

He was brought up before the judge, the same one with whom I had consulted, and one of the most severe legal contests followed I ever witnesed. John Jay, Esq., son of Judge Jay, then a young lawyer, was first employed in the case. Two other lawyers volunteered to assist in the case. There is a law in

New York which requires the district attorney, on being notified that a citizen's liberty is in danger, to appear and defend him, subjecting him to a heavy fine and imprisonment if he fails to do so. Mr. Jay served the required notice upon Mr. M'Keon, the district attorney of the county and city of New York, who was a very able lawyer, but a life-long Democrat. This gave us four lawyers.

Mr. M'Keon appeared and took the lead. In opening the case he said: " Your Honor must know that I am not here from choice; I have been summoned here under a law which not only makes it my official duty to appear in the case, but subjects me to heavy penalties in case of neglect or refusal. Such being my relation to the case, your honor will expect me to do my duty." And he did his duty; more, he displayed wonders of skill, tact, and cunning. The points involved only can be stated.

A planter from Maryland appeared as claimant, with an equal array of council.

The nephew of the claimant was introduced as a witness, by whom it was proved that the colored man was his slave, that he had known him from his childhood, that he was born on his uncle's plantation, and had always lived there as his slave until he disappeared recently. No one doubted the truth of the facts sworn to, but the effort was to evade the legal consequences.

Mr. M'Keon denied that Maryland was a slave-

holding State.   While he admitted that the evidence
proved the man to have been held as a slave, it did
not prove that he was lawfully held, which could not
be proved by parole testimony; the law itself must be
produced. This at first was thought to be only a
vexatious quibble, for it was supposed to be an easy
matter to produce a volume of Maryland laws, but it
soon became serious.   Resort was first made to the
great law library which contained the laws of all the
States, but no copy of Maryland laws could be found.
Messengers flew from one private law library to
another without success.   Finally a messenger came,
all out of breath, with a volume of Maryland laws,
and it was supposed the case was settled. Counsel rose
with the open volume in hand to read to the court,
when Mr. M'Keon objected. He denied that that
book contained the laws of Maryland, and demanded
the certificate of the Secretary of the State. The
judge finally decided that they might prove the book
by parole testimony if they could, but that was no
easy matter. One of our counsel had practiced law
in Baltimore and they put him on the stand.

To the question, " Have you practiced law in the
State of Maryland ? " he answered, " Yes." " Have
you got the laws of Maryland ? " He answered, " I
had them, but have not got them now ; some person
has stolen them from me."

Showing him the volume which had been brought
in, " Is not this your book ? "

Looking at it he answered, "This is not my book; mine had my name in it."

"Is that the Laws of Maryland?"

"It looks very much like the volume of Maryland laws, but I cannot say it is." That was all they could make him say.

Just at this point one of the counsel for the claimant found in the enactments of the last session of the Legislature one which said, "Books claiming upon their face to be the laws of other States, published by the authority of the State, may be read in the courts of this State without further proof." No reference to such a case as this was intended in the passage of that act; yet it covered the case, and it appeared lost. I could read in the face of Mr. M'Keon that he thought it was lost. Before he could rally, if he could have rallied at all, the judge called out, "Hand me that book." It was reached up to him. Having glanced his eye over the title-page he said, "Our statute says, 'Published by the authority of the State.' This book reads, 'Published by authority;' it does not say what authority. I decide that it is insufficient; the man must be discharged."

The excitement had become very great, and many people had gathered in the park around the Courthouse who could not get in, and many police officers were sent there to keep order. They formed a line two deep, reaching from the door of the court-room to the street gate. These were all ready to enforce the

orders of the court; and the decision went out and
was known outside before there was any special move
within. When the judge ordered the man discharged
counsel requested the court to detain him until they
could make out papers for his arrest as a fugitive
slave; but the judge declined, saying it was not in accordance with his taste to do so. Already the pen was
at work to draft the necessary papers for a legal arrest. Mr. M'Keon turned to the young man, and said,
" You are free, and your legs are the only security that
you will remain free." He did not need another hint,
and he shot from the room with the speed of an
arrow, and word of his discharge having passed out
ahead of him, the police opened, and he ran between
two rows of police reaching to the gate, who, with all
the multitude, shouted till the welkin rang. The
slave-holder in the court-room trembled, believing
it was the shout of a mob who would lynch him,
and he requested the court to grant him a police
guard to protect him to his hotel. While the judge
granted his request he assured him that not one of
those men would injure a hair of his head.

In the spring of 1852 I removed from the city of
New York to the city of Syracuse, where, during a
three-years' pastorate, I did the largest work of my
life on the Under-ground Railroad. I passed as many
as thirty slaves through my hands in a month. There
were reasons why the business flourished in my hands.
The terrors of the Fugitive Slave Law sent them all

through to Canada. They formerly stopped on this side, but now no one felt safe until he stood on British soil. Syracuse was a convenient shipping-point. I could put them in a car and tell them to keep their seats until they crossed the suspension bridge, and then they would be in Canada.

The most potent reason was, doubtless, the fact that it cost nothing to ship fugitive slaves from Syracuse to Canada. From all other points their fare had to be paid; if they could get to Syracuse they went free the rest of the way. The fact was, I had friends, or the slave had, connected with the railroad at Syracuse, of whom I never failed to get a free pass in this form: "Pass this poor colored man," or "poor colored woman," or "poor colored family," as the case might be. The conductors on the route understood these passes, and they were never challenged.

My name, the name of my street, and the number of my residence, came to be known as far south as Baltimore, and I did a large business. Many cases were of thrilling interest, but it will not do to report them, as they would make a book. I will only show my surroundings—how I was backed by the community. To give a clear view of things I must notice the Jerry rescue, which occurred while I resided in the city of New York, and with which I had nothing to do at the time. Jerry was a fugitive slave residing in Syracuse. It was soon after the passage of the Fugitive Slave Law. Mr. Daniel Webster passed through Syracuse, and made a speech in which he said the Fugitive Slave Law was part of an important compromise which the interest of the whole nation required, and they must conquer their prejudices and enforce it. " Yes," said he, " it will be enforced in Syracuse during the next session of your county antislavery convention." It so came to pass that during the next county antislavery convention Jerry was arrested. The investigation was protracted until night, and then Jerry was rescued. There was an attempt made to punish the rescuers, and a number of persons were arrested; but they did not get the right men. A Mr. Cobb was put upon trial, and they proved by positive testimony that he turned the gas off, and but for one plucky Irishman on the jury he would have been convicted; and yet Mr. Cobb had nothing to do with it. It was a case of mistaken identity. The man who turned the gas off was an entire stranger in the city, but of the same style of man and dress as Mr. Cobb. The moment he had done the deed he jumped upon a train of cars and went directly to the city of New York, and in a few hours was where I might have put my hand upon him.

When I returned to Syracuse in 1852 I found determined opposition to the Fugitive Slave Law. They celebrated the anniversary of the Jerry rescue, and I was called upon for an address among others; and I was radical enough to come up to their standard. When it was found that I was engaged on the Under-ground Railroad I had good supporters, and enough of them, and I did a large business.

Precaution was taken against any surprise by slave-catching officers. A signal was arranged. A particular ring of a very far-sounding bell in the Congregational church told the people for four and five miles that help was wanted for a fugitive slave, and they would come rushing down from Onondaga Hills in a manner that meant business.

There was a gentleman—one of our true men—by the name of Obed Miner. He left town to go as far west as Lyons on business, and a telegram was received, sent from Lyons, as follows :

"There will be a fugitive slave on the train which will pass Syracuse at eight o'clock this evening.
"(Signed,)   O. M."

A consultation was held. All knew that if the "O. M." represented Obed Miner there was business to be attended to, but most believed it to be a game of our enemies ; but it was thought best to be on the safe side, and at the right time the bell sent its pealing call, thrilling the air for miles. The result was, when the train arrived there were a thousand men on the track, and the way into the depot was closed up. The conductor, learning what the demonstration meant, came out upon the platform and stated that, upon his honor, there was no slave on board of his train, and that he would not carry a fugitive back to bondage.

The throng opened to the right and left, and the train rolled into the depot and the people went quietly to their homes; and the pro-slavery men were convinced that it would not do to arrest a fugitive slave in Syracuse, or to carry one through the city if it were known.

Not long before I left the city two persons were arrested in Milwaukee, under the Fugitive Slave Law, for having assisted the escape of slaves. A meeting of sympathy was called in Syracuse, and speeches were made and resolutions adopted. His honor the mayor presided, and made a speech on taking the chair. He stated that he had always been conservative, but he could not endure the Fugitive Slave Law. He had heard much said about the Under-ground Railroad, but he was now in favor of laying the track above ground and he was willing to help defend it there.

Several speeches were made, and I was called for the last speech. It was getting late, the people were weary, and I must strike boldly or fail. I planted my feet on the rock of eternal right. I affirmed that slavery is wrong—a moral wrong, a violation of every commandment of the decalogue, that no law can make it right to practice it, support it, or to in any way aid and abet it; that the Fugitive Slave Law is a war upon God, upon his law, and upon the rights of humanity; that to obey it, or to aid in its enforcement, is treason against God and humanity, and involves a guilt equal to the guilt of violating every one of the ten commandments. I never had obeyed it—I never would obey it. I had assisted thirty slaves to escape to Canada during the last month. If the United States authorities wanted any thing of me my residence was at 39 Onondaga-street. I would admit that they could take me and lock me up in the Penitentiary on the hill; but if they did such a foolish thing as that I had friends enough in Onondaga County to level it with the ground before the next morning.

The immense throng rose upon their feet and shouted, " We will do it ! we will do it !" and I have no doubt at that moment they thought they would.

This chapter narrates but a small part of my labors on the Under-ground Railroad, but it will give a good view of the spirit and perils of those times. I am thankful I never did turn away from helping a fugitive slave, and I remember with gratitude the readiness with which others always responded to my calls for help. The business I transacted in Syracuse, in conducting the Under-ground Railroad, often cost money, and it was always furnished when I called for it. When money was wanting to clothe, feed, or help a slave in any way, I only had to say so to a friend, and it came without further effort on my part.

CHAPTER XLIII.

A Review of Life—Its Evening Hour—In Sight of the Crossing—The Prospect Beyond.

AS men usually compute time, my life has been a long one. In a few days I shall be eighty-one years old. But what are eighty-one years when past? They may be something in deeds, good or bad, and may be great in responsibility, for "God requireth that which is past;" but as mere duration they are insignificant. When I was young, time looked almost like a forever to the period when I should be eighty; but now the years are gone, and as I look back upon them, the whole looks like a departed day or a faded hour. The whole career of life, with all its activities and successes and failures, seems but little more than a troubled dream imperfectly remembered.

But when I undertake to analyze life, and count out its dark and troubled days, and its bright, sunny hours, and number its many trials and temptations, and the deliverances; when I attempt to locate the many battle-grounds, and offset the victories and defeats against each other, and weigh the joys and sorrows, and measure out the several weary stages, it is no empty dream. I then deal with realities. It is then that I see how much rugged way I have passed,

22

how many rocky hills I have crossed, how many narrow defiles I have threaded, and how many slippery precipices I have walked, when an unseen hand must have led me safely, or I had slipped, fallen, and perished. I see many dark sorrows overhanging part of the way, and I count the graves of many dear friends as I look back over the road I have traveled.

But life has not all been dark and rough; there are seen along the way some bright spots, here and there a fountain, around which an oasis bloomed, giving a happy resting-place for a few days or a few hours. Remembered joys, which blessed the years that have fled, are like the chime we hear from a far-off dome, floating on the zephyrs of a summer evening's twilight hour. No remembered joys of earth are so dear as those that blessed the humble abode of the itinerant, now seen far back by the way-side, when children caroled in my home. Thought wanders back, and my ears hear those clattering little feet and voices, and my heart bounds at the remembered greetings when I returned, weary and care-worn, from my toils abroad. These visions last only for a moment; the spell is broken, and I awake to a realization of the fact that those joys were known in the distant past, and are forever gone.

> Sweet are those joys remembered long,
>   The joys that blest the days of yore;
> But sweeter far now past and gone,
>   To come and bless my home no more.

From cottage floor, along life's track,
  The voices of loved children thrill;
And swift-winged thought oft wanders back,
  And listens to those voices still.

Soft echoes from those distant years,
  Like muffled chimes from far-off dome,
Still breathe sweet music in my ears,
  Of childhood's carols in my home.

But silent now my cottage door,
  No children's voices greet my ears;
For children carol there no more
  As in those long-departed years.

But how short has life been! The reader starts and inquires, Has life been short to one who has lived eighty years? Yes, eighty years, when past, are but a few short years. When I first woke up to the fact that I was an old man I could not understand how I had become so old in so short a time. I might never have understood the matter, had not my Muse whispered the secret in my ear:

But just beyond life's dark and troubled years
The sunny morn of childhood still appears,
And thought flies back, once more to quaff the joy,
To join the play, or sport again the toy.

But childhood's hours, so full of heartsome glee,
Were born with wings and waited not for me;
As flits the shadow of a bird away,
So childhood vanished while I was at play.

I was a youth, with garlands on my brow,
Not as I am, a care-worn pilgrim, now;
Life throbbed in every vein, and beat the heart
With zeal, to act in life a noble part.

But years went by, as years had gone before;
Youth felt their touch, and youth was youth no more,
So quickly changed by time's transforming power,
Departed youth seemed but a faded hour.

The years of manhood, active, brave, and strong,
Were given to the right, against the wrong;
Then Truth and Error met upon the field,
And long the battle raged—Truth would not yield.

And so intensely earnest was the fight,
Quite unperceived Time made his rapid flight,
Till age had gathered on the warrior's brow,
And white his locks, just as you see them now.

The fact that I have grown so old in what appears to be so short a time finds its explanation in the extreme activity and earnestness of my life, which caused me to make little note of time. Amid the activities of a busy, earnest day, we have but little time to think beyond what engages us as the hours pass; but when the evening comes, with its relaxation and stillness, we can review the deeds and results of the whole day with calmness, scrutiny, and profit. I am now enjoying life's quiet evening hour, and can take a more calm, reflective, and impartial view of life than I could in the midst of its earnest activities. I thank God for this calm hour, and feel that it is a great blessing to enjoy it at the close of so long, active, and stern a life as mine has been. The storms and battles of life are ended, and I have time to review the whole and sum up the results.

If I estimated life by the worldly advantages I

have secured for myself, I should pronounce it a failure. Mine has been a life of hard labor, full of anxiety and solicitude, and yet it has secured me neither riches, position, nor fame. My life closes as it began, with very little of this world; indeed, not enough to insure me against want in helpless old age. I really believe I might have secured wealth had I devoted myself to it as ardently as I did to what I believed to be truth and righteousness. This course was not pursued because I was indifferent to wealth. I never saw the day when I would not have secured wealth could I have done it in harmony with my convictions of duty; but that was impossible. The course which I believed it my duty to pursue would bring me neither popularity, wealth, nor many friends; and so I have lived and come down to old age without them. During all my life have I maintained a war against both the sale and use of intoxicating drinks. This I did when it cost something, when I had to contend with local preachers, stewards, class-leaders, and members on the charges to which I was appointed, and it sometimes made my loaf of bread smaller than it would otherwise have been. Thirty years of the prime of my life were almost exclusively devoted to the overthrow of the accursed system of slavery, in the face of opposition from the Church and the world, from priests and politicians. This warfare, waged for conscience' sake, secured for me more poverty than money, and more enemies than friends.

But I do not regard life a failure because I have not secured the highest advantages of this world. If I have done something to advance the cause of temperance to its present strength, and if I have contributed to the overthrow of slavery, life has been no failure. But in another aspect life has been a success. I have preserved my integrity, and come out of life's struggle an honest man, having never sold myself for place or pelf. I wish here to record the fact that this is all my boast; I claim nothing for myself more than the honor of having lived an honest man. Nor do unsupplied wants in old age tempt me to regret the course I have pursued. If I now had wealth, place, and powerful friends, I could enjoy them but a short time; and if they were the price of integrity, if to gain them I had suppressed one utterance of God's truth when it was called for, they would cloud life's setting sun, and make death less welcome, if they would not plant my dying bed with thorns. It is better to die in a poor-house, true and honest, than to die surrounded by friends and luxuries purchased at the expense of integrity.

More than eighty years old, and yet my heart feels young; and I am not infirm, as must be known from the fact that I am in the habit of going from home and addressing large congregations morning and evening. Last June I visited Lake Superior, seven hundred miles from my home, and preached and lectured through the copper region for two months, speaking from four to six times a week, and all this without a traveling companion. Yet, when I remember that I was born in 1800, I know I am old and cannot tarry here much longer.

It is not the most cheering thought that after a long life and severe struggle I must leave the world just as its salvation is beginning to dawn; yet this chilling thought is relieved by a brighter one. The cause of God will experience no shock or check when I drop out; God will provide agencies, who, under him, will carry it on successfully.

It has been a great privilege to live in such an age as I have lived in. Every thing which is now classed among modern improvements has been brought out for trial in my day. Steamboats, railroads, telegraphs, the power-press, paper-making machines, all manner of labor-saving machines, have been invented and brought out in my time. I was ten years old when the first cotton-thread was spun by machinery in the United States.

All the civilizing, moralizing, Christianizing, and elevating institutions beyond the simple Church which are hastening the world's salvation have been born of the wisdom and benevolence which have blessed the years of my short life. The great Bible societies of Europe and America are younger than I am, and so are all the great missionary organizations. More has been done for the elevation of humanity and the salvation of the world since I was born than was done in the preceding thousand years. As late as when I commenced my ministry the Methodist Episcopal Church had only seventeen Annual Conferences, including all the Southern States and Canada. Now there are ninety-four Conferences, exclusive of the Church South and Canada, besides foreign work. Such has been the increase of the Methodist Episcopal Church during my ministry; and the fact that I have contributed to these results in the smallest degree is worth my life of toil.

Old age has a shady side, if we will allow ourselves to dwell in the shade. When I first realized that I was an old man I read a poem which contained these lines:

> "The winds of time have swept
> Long since my youth and manhood's prime away,
> And through my frame a withering blight has crept,
> The mildew of decay."

A shadow seemed to come over me for a moment when I read these lines, but it was only for a moment. The end of life would be dark indeed if there were no vision and no hope beyond the grave, but Christ has "abolished death, and brought life and immortality to light through the Gospel." As I look down into the grave now open at my feet I hear the voice of Christ saying, "I am the resurrection, and the life: he that believeth in me, though he were dead, yet shall he live: and whosoever liveth and believeth in me shall never die."

The Gospel which I have preached to others for sixty years is now my light, and it sheds its brightness upon my evening hour of life, as hill-tops are bathed in glory by the last rays of the setting sun while shadows gather at their base.

A care-worn pilgrim, still I roam,
  Far down the vale, hard by the shore,
And wait, where Jordan's waters foam,
  The mystic boat to bear me o'er.

My sun goes down, the west is clear;
  Bright golden beams athwart the sky
Proclaim the gates of heaven near
  I know the entrance must be nigh.

The evening glow of golden hue
  Is flashed from heaven's outer shrine;
But, pass the inner veil once through,
  The glory will be all divine.

Jehovah there his face unvails,
  And glory covers all the plain;
It lights the hills, illumes the vales,
  His temple all—our living fane.

Why tremble, then, so near the gate,
  And fear to leave this world of sin,
While angels at the portals wait
  To welcome weary pilgrims in?

THE END.

TITLES in THIS SERIES

geles, 1925), *AROUND THE WORLD BY FAITH, WITH SIX WEEKS IN THE HOLY LAND* (Los Angeles, n. d.), *TWO YEARS MISSION WORK IN EUROPE JUST BEFORE THE WORLD WAR, 1912-14* (Los Angeles, [1926])

6. Boardman, W. E., *THE HIGHER CHRISTIAN LIFE* (Boston, 1858)

7. Girvin, E. A., *PHINEAS F. BRESEE: A PRINCE IN ISRAEL* (Kansas City, Mo., [1916])

8. Brooks, John P., *THE DIVINE CHURCH* (Columbia, Mo., 1891)

9. RUSSELL KELSO CARTER ON "FAITH HEALING." R. Kelso Carter, *THE ATONEMENT FOR SIN AND SICKNESS* (Boston, 1884) *"FAITH HEALING" REVIEWED AFTER TWENTY YEARS* (Boston, 1897)

10. Daniels, W. H., *DR. CULLIS AND HIS WORK* (Boston, [1885])

11. HOLINESS TRACTS DEFENDING THE MINISTRY OF WOMEN. Luther Lee, *"WOMAN'S RIGHT TO PREACH THE GOSPEL; A SERMON, AT THE ORDINATION OF REV. MISS ANTOINETTE L. BROWN, AT SOUTH BUTLER, WAYNE COUNTY, N. Y., SEPT. 15, 1853"* (Syracuse, 1853) *bound with* B. T. Roberts, *ORDAINING WOMEN* (Rochester, 1891) *bound with* Catherine (Mumford) Booth, *"FEMALE MINISTRY; OR, WOMAN'S RIGHT TO PREACH THE GOSPEL . . ."* (London, n. d.) *bound with* Fannie (McDowell) Hunter, *WOMEN PREACHERS* (Dallas, 1905)

12. LATE NINETEENTH CENTURY REVIVALIST TEACHINGS ON THE HOLY SPIRIT. D. L. Moody, *SECRET POWER OR THE SECRET OF SUCCESS IN CHRISTIAN LIFE AND*

WORK (New York, [1881]) *bound with* J. Wilbur Chapman, RECEIVED YE THE HOLY GHOST? (New York, [1894]) *bound with* R. A. Torrey, THE BAPTISM WITH THE HOLY SPIRIT (New York, 1895 & 1897)

13. SEVEN "JESUS ONLY" TRACTS. Andrew D. Urshan, *THE DOCTRINE OF THE NEW BIRTH, OR, THE PERFECT WAY TO ETERNAL LIFE* (Cochrane, Wis., 1921) *bound with* Andrew Urshan, *THE ALMIGHTY GOD IN THE LORD JESUS CHRIST* (Los Angeles, 1919) *bound with* Frank J. Ewart, *THE REVELATION OF JESUS CHRIST* (St. Louis, n. d.) *bound with* G. T. Haywood, *THE BIRTH OF THE SPIRIT IN THE DAYS OF THE APOSTLES* (Indianapolis, n. d.) *DIVINE NAMES AND TITLES OF JEHOVAH* (Indianapolis, n. d.) *THE FINEST OF THE WHEAT* (Indianapolis, n. d.) *THE VICTIM OF THE FLAMING SWORD* (Indianapolis, n. d.)

14. THREE EARLY PENTECOSTAL TRACTS. D. Wesley Myland, *THE LATTER RAIN COVENANT AND PENTECOSTAL POWER* (Chicago, 1910) *bound with* G. F. Taylor, *THE SPIRIT AND THE BRIDE* (n. p., [1907?]) *bound with* B. F. Laurence, *THE APOSTOLIC FAITH RESTORED* (St. Louis, 1916)

15. Fairchild, James H., *OBERLIN: THE COLONY AND THE COLLEGE, 1833-1883* (Oberlin, 1883)

16. Figgis, John B., *KESWICK FROM WITHIN* (London, [1914])

17. Finney, Charles G., *LECTURES TO PROFESSING CHRISTIANS* (New York, 1837)

18. Fleisch, Paul, *DIE MODERNE GEMEINSCHAFTSBEWEGUNG IN DEUTSCHLAND* (Leipzig, 1912)

19. SIX TRACTS BY W. B. GODBEY. *SPIRITUAL GIFTS AND GRACES* (Cincinnati, [1895]) *THE RETURN OF JESUS* (Cincinnati, [1899?]) *WORK OF THE HOLY SPIRIT* (Louisville, [1902]) *CHURCH—BRIDE—KINGDOM* (Cincinnati, [1905]) *DIVINE HEALING* (Greensboro, [1909]) *TONGUE MOVEMENT, SATANIC* (Zarephath, N. J., 1918)

20. Gordon, Earnest B., *ADONIRAM JUDSON GORDON* (New York, [1896])

21. Hills, A. M., *HOLINESS AND POWER FOR THE CHURCH AND THE MINISTRY* (Cincinnati, [1897])

22. Horner, Ralph C., *FROM THE ALTAR TO THE UPPER ROOM* (Toronto, [1891])

23. McDonald, William and John E. Searles, *THE LIFE OF REV. JOHN S. INSKIP* (Boston, [1885])

24. LaBerge, Agnes N. O:, *WHAT GOD HATH WROUGHT* (Chicago, n. d.)

25. Lee, Luther, *AUTOBIOGRAPHY OF THE REV. LUTHER LEE* (New York, 1882)

26. McLean, A. and J. W. Easton, *PENUEL; OR, FACE TO FACE WITH GOD* (New York, 1869)

27. McPherson, Aimee Semple, *THIS IS THAT: PERSONAL EXPERIENCES SERMONS AND WRITINGS* (Los Angeles, [1919])

28. Mahan, Asa, *OUT OF DARKNESS INTO LIGHT* (London, 1877)

29. THE LIFE AND TEACHING OF CARRIE JUDD MONTGOMERY Carrie Judd Montgomery, *"UNDER HIS WINGS": THE STORY OF MY LIFE* (Oakland,

[1936]) Carrie F. Judd, *THE PRAYER OF FAITH* (New York, 1880)

30. THE DEVOTIONAL WRITINGS OF PHOEBE PALMER Phoebe Palmer, *THE WAY OF HOLINESS* (52nd ed., New York, 1867) *FAITH AND ITS EFFECTS* (27th ed., New York, n. d., orig. pub. 1854)

31. Wheatley, Richard, *THE LIFE AND LETTERS OF MRS. PHOEBE PALMER* (New York, 1881)

32. Palmer, Phoebe, ed., *PIONEER EXPERIENCES* (New York, 1868)

33. Palmer, Phoebe, *THE PROMISE OF THE FATHER* (Boston, 1859)

34. Pardington, G. P., *TWENTY-FIVE WONDERFUL YEARS, 1889-1914: A POPULAR SKETCH OF THE CHRISTIAN AND MISSIONARY ALLIANCE* (New York, [1914])

35. Parham, Sarah E., *THE LIFE OF CHARLES F. PARHAM, FOUNDER OF THE APOSTOLIC FAITH MOVEMENT* (Joplin, [1930])

36. THE SERMONS OF CHARLES F. PARHAM. Charles F. Parham, *A VOICE CRYING IN THE WILDERNESS* (4th ed., Baxter Springs, Kan., 1944, orig. pub. 1902) *THE EVERLASTING GOSPEL* (n.p., n.d., orig. pub. 1911)

37. Pierson, Arthur Tappan, *FORWARD MOVEMENTS OF THE LAST HALF CENTURY* (New York, 1905)

38. *PROCEEDINGS OF HOLINESS CONFERENCES, HELD AT CINCINNATI, NOVEMBER 26TH, 1877, AND AT NEW YORK, DECEMBER 17TH, 1877* (Philadelphia, 1878)

39. *RECORD OF THE CONVENTION FOR THE PROMOTION OF*

SCRIPTURAL HOLINESS HELD AT BRIGHTON, MAY 29TH, TO JUNE 7TH, 1875 (Brighton, [1896?])

40. Rees, Seth Cook, MIRACLES IN THE SLUMS (Chicago, [1905?])

41. Roberts, B. T., WHY ANOTHER SECT (Rochester, 1879)

42. Shaw, S. B., ed., ECHOES OF THE GENERAL HOLINESS ASSEMBLY (Chicago, [1901])

43. THE DEVOTIONAL WRITINGS OF ROBERT PEARSALL SMITH AND HANNAH WHITALL SMITH. [R]obert [P]earsall [S]mith, HOLINESS THROUGH FAITH: LIGHT ON THE WAY OF HOLINESS (New York, [1870]) [H]annah [W]hitall [S]mith, THE CHRISTIAN'S SECRET OF A HAPPY LIFE, (Boston and Chicago, [1885])

44. [S]mith, [H]annah [W]hitall, THE UNSELFISHNESS OF GOD AND HOW I DISCOVERED IT (New York, [1903])

45. Steele, Daniel, A SUBSTITUTE FOR HOLINESS; OR, ANTINOMIANISM REVIVED (Chicago and Boston, [1899])

46. Tomlinson, A. J., THE LAST GREAT CONFLICT (Cleveland, 1913)

47. Upham, Thomas C., THE LIFE OF FAITH (Boston, 1845)

48. Washburn, Josephine M., HISTORY AND REMINISCENCES OF THE HOLINESS CHURCH WORK IN SOUTHERN CALIFORNIA AND ARIZONA (South Pasadena, [1912?])